A Company of Citizens

A Company of
Citizens

WHAT THE WORLD'S FIRST DEMOCRACY
TEACHES LEADERS ABOUT CREATING
GREAT ORGANIZATIONS

Brook Manville
Josiah Ober

HARVARD BUSINESS SCHOOL PRESS
BOSTON, MASSACHUSETTS

Library of Congress Cataloging-in-Publication Data

Manville, Brook, 1950–
    A company of citizens : what the world's first democracy teaches
leaders about creating great organization / Brook Manville, Josiah Ober.
        p. cm.
Includes index.
    ISBN 1-57851-440-1
    1. Organizational behavior. 2. Management. 3. Citizenship. 4. Democracy.
5. Corporate governance. I. Ober, Josiah. II. Title.
    HD58.7 .M3714 2003
    658—dc21

                                                            2002151059

The paper used in this publication meets the requirements of the American
National Standard for Permanence of Paper for Publications and Documents
in Libraries and Archives Z39.48–1992.

For Adrienne and Margarita
and
For Laura, Martin, and Sabrina

Contents

Preface

THIS BOOK is the result of a decade of conversations between the authors and their colleagues about what it means to be a member of an organization. The conversations ran along three parallel tracks: the increasing "democratization" of the workplace, the growing importance of "human capital" and learning in the global economy, and the underappreciated organizational genius of citizenship in the ancient Greek city-state of Athens. The convergence of those three tracks led us to write the story that follows. We began to appreciate that much of what the Athenians had originally invented—the alignment of individual excellence and community focus through a sophisticated model of self-governing citizens—was surprisingly appropriate to new ways of working in the Knowledge Age, an era in which people, what they know, and how well they learn from and collaborate with one another have become the key differentiators for organizational success. We realized that even the best current discussions about workplace democracy tended to be based upon inappropriate, modern Western notions of democracy as an impersonal form of representative government. We knew that the ancient Greek concept of democracy as a passionate commitment was both less well-known to leaders and more directly relevant to contemporary debates about the "organization of the future."

This book is written for leaders—a term that we use to encompass not only company CEOs and senior managers, but also thought leaders, team leaders, and indeed everyone who leads work while also seeking to shape his or her own destiny in the modern workplace. Leaders of every kind are in constant need of models and metaphors to help them better understand the changing world around them, and to stimulate their thinking about how to manage for the challenges that lie ahead. The premise of this book is that the Athenian approach to organizing people— as self-governing, knowledge-sharing citizens—reflects a valuable, timely, and practical model for engaging, aligning, and motivating workers in today's Knowledge Age. We believe that knowledge workers increasingly expect certain rights in exchange for taking on responsibilities, and seek to be members of firms that support their own core values of freedom and equality. They are ready, in brief, to be citizens of their organizations: passionate sharers in the business of ruling, leaders who also understand how to follow.

The practical usefulness of the Athenian citizenship model was demonstrated in 1998, when we were invited to join a project team involved in rethinking the governance structure of a large professional services firm. The firm, originally founded as an informal self-governing partnership, had grown considerably over the years and was quickly drifting toward becoming a corporate hierarchy of a very conventional sort. Our assignment was to determine whether a coherent approach to governance could be devised that would provide a more formal structure while still preserving the firm's original open culture and prerogatives of partnership. After conducting a series of interviews and discussions with the firm's partners and considering a variety of governance alternatives, our team fastened upon the ancient Athenian model of democratic community. We devised a solution that adapted many of the ancient Greek institutions and processes to the modern governance and culture of the firm. The proposal was enthusiastically embraced by the partners, one of whom described the proposed solution, after its presentation at a worldwide conference, as a "distinctive and forward-looking solution that at the same time took the firm back to its roots."

Meanwhile, we discovered that no less an authority than Charles Handy had been ruminating on some of the same ideas. Also in 1998, he published a thoughtful essay entitled "The Citizen Company" which argued that the concept of citizenship is a "force that organizations must now come to terms with as their individuals begin to expect from their work communities the same collection of freedoms, rights, and responsibilities that they have in the wider society."[1] Handy's discussion is an inspiring and provocative challenge to traditional thinking; but it remains only a sketch of a topic that we knew from our own work to be extraordinarily rich and complex. This book builds on Handy's insight that the workers of a company should be regarded as its citizens, while drawing on our own distinctive belief that the richest and most appropriate model for company citizenship is the humanistic and vibrant version of classical democracy. The pages that follow make this argument, explaining how a leader today can take advantage of timeless ancient lessons and apply Athenian principles to building a modern company of citizens. Our conviction in the potential value of doing so has been strengthened by the opportunities we have had recently to apply those principles in other practical situations and consulting assignments.

In developing our model, based on the case study of an ancient organization, we have focused on the specific aspects of

Athenian history that we believe will be most relevant for today's leaders. That meant leaving out a lot of detail and skipping over scholarly debates that have raged for decades or more. We assure our readers that we do know the historical detail and the scholarly debates; we have each previously written well-received books and articles about ancient Athenian democracy for demanding academic audiences. Readers who become interested enough in the Athenian model for its own sake, and who want to know more about the details and academic controversies, will find relevant references in our endnotes, which cite some of the most important modern scholarship on ancient Greek history, as well as related work on organizational theory and practice. In addition to modern works, we reference a number of ancient Greek writers; these are cited according to the ordinary conventions of historical scholarship (usually by author, work, book number, and section number). Translations of Greek writers are either our own, or adapted from what we regard as the most reliable and readable modern translations.

Like all good collaborations, this effort of joint authorship has sought to combine different yet complementary skills and perspectives. The synthesis we offer is the result of much reading and debate, lessons learned in the crucibles of practice, a certain amount of compromise between the perspectives and cultures of the academic and business worlds, and a lot of hard work writing and rewriting. In the end, our thinking became so thoroughly interwoven that it is impossible for us to assign individual authorship for any given section, although Ober held greatest sway in ancient history and democratic theory and Manville in organizational theory and the implications of the case for modern application. Needless to say, we take shared responsibility for all that follows.

ACKNOWLEDGMENTS

We impute no responsibility, but offer our heartfelt thanks to the many people who advised us, commented on our work, and challenged us to push deeper into our project along the way. This book would be very different and much worse but for the acute insights provided by friends and colleagues who took time to read earlier drafts, brainstorm ideas, and discuss with us everything from the central theses to the practical implications to the details of our prose. A book so long in the making inevitably benefits from hundreds of helping hands, but those people we would particularly like to acknowledge are as follows: consultant colleagues Ian Davis, John Ferejohn, Steve Hong, Larry Kanarek, Jon Katzenbach, Jürgen Kluge, Bill Meehan, and Bill Snyder; reviewers Tom Davenport, Douglas K. Smith, and Etienne Wenger; and other friends and colleagues who read portions, commented on ideas, and advised us along the way, including Christopher Bartlett, Jim Collins, Nathaniel Foote, Andrew Ford, Jennifer Futernick, Byron Henderson, David Johnson, Adrienne Mayor, Jeffrey Pfeffer, Michael Schrage, Barry Strauss, Bob Sutton, and Alan Webber. Ober would also like to give special thanks to the students of his fall 2001 Princeton seminars on the circulation of knowledge and participatory democracy; they helped to extend and refine our ancient-modern parallels. Manville offers his gratitude to a host of Saba Software colleagues (especially founder and CEO Bobby Yazdani) whose discussions about the "human capital revolution" did much to inform our thinking.

This project would never have seen the light of day without our editors at Harvard Business School Press, particularly Hollis Heimbouch. As a visionary acquiring editor, she saw that there was a book lurking in our ideas, and as a disciplined developmental editor, she forced us to "get it right." Thanks also to Genoveva Llosa, who supported and challenged us throughout the long editorial process.

Finally, our deepest gratitude to the people who sacrificed most in the course of the long gestation of this book: our families. Both of our wives and Manville's children have patiently put up with the many hours that writing this book has demanded; we dedicate it to all of them.

PRINCETON, NEW JERSEY
WASHINGTON, D.C.

A Company of Citizens

CHAPTER I

Back to the Future

IMAGINE GREECE. What do you see in your mind's eye? Sandy beaches, lively tavernas, perhaps a bronze statue of an ancient hero. And yet, even if you've never been to Greece, these are soon eclipsed by a more powerful image: the soaring columns of a gleaming marble building, perched high on a barren hill above a bustling modern city—the Parthenon. The people of ancient Athens built this, the world's most famous Greek temple, and dedicated it to the goddess of wisdom some 2,400 years ago. Today it remains a breathtaking artifact of artistic achievement and a timeless symbol of outstanding organizational performance.

The power of the Parthenon image begins with its beauty and grandeur: "the most remarkable building in the world," in the opinion of some modern architectural experts.[1] The entire edifice was made of marble, an unprecedented construction with a stone notoriously difficult to quarry, transport, and sculpt. Attention to detail in the Parthenon was also unprecedented, and its architectural design was truly pioneering, with a multitude of subtle optical refinements, the result of "unparalleled mathematical precision."[2] Architects and engineers constructed the floor as ever so slightly convex, with each column also bulging slightly in the center. The artisans realized that in the brilliant light of the Mediterranean sun the human eye plays tricks, adds concavity to horizontals, perceives vertical elements as thinner than they really are—and thus they designed a monument that corrected for the illusion and created a building that shines forth with perfectly proportioned dynamism and grace.

The Parthenon was incredibly expensive to build—roughly the equivalent of half a billion dollars today. And the temple was built to house an even more precious artifact: an ivory and gold statue of the patron goddess Athena, valued at twice the cost of the entire building. Yet the money that went into the Parthenon project represented only a fraction of Athenian wealth, generated by an extensive empire that stretched across the Aegean Sea, consisting of some 200 smaller states and islands. A powerful navy enforced tribute and allegiance to Athens, and the empire was administered by the citizen democracy of all Athenians. The capital resources that enabled the Athenians to build the Parthenon and maintain this empire were not limited to money alone; a deep reserve of knowledge and skills was required as well. Through its networks of relationships, its reputation for excellence, and its ability to generate growth, the citizen organization of Athens attracted talented people from across the Mediterranean world—men and women who flocked to a city renowned for openness and opportunity. The Athenians uniquely learned how to take full advantage of this bounty of human talent. They did so as a highly focused moral community of entrepreneurial individuals—a company of citizens.

Although the stones have outlasted the institutional structure of the self-governing city, the Athenians' individual-centered values of freedom and equality remain profoundly influential today, and Athenian democracy itself stands as a shining example of the resilience of an organization based on a culture of citizenship. During the nearly two centuries of its independent existence as a democratic community, Athens was repeatedly challenged for its very survival. The Athenians fought major wars, built and lost an empire, suffered defeats and confronted constitutional crises—always to bounce back, recovering their prosperity and expanding their reputation for innovation. The self-governing democracy and the citizen culture were the engines of this amazingly durable and flexible adaptiveness to change.

For modern visitors, the Parthenon speaks of serenity and strength. Yet for the ancient Greeks it also spoke of extraordinary organizational speed and agility. Unlike most major Greek building projects, which spanned multiple generations, this temple, "as near perfection as human handiwork is likely to go," was built in only nine years.[3] It was also built during a period of ongoing military conflict with Athens' most powerful rivals, and revolts in parts of their empire. The beautiful temple thus also symbolizes an unusual ability on the part of the citizen community to assemble and flexibly deploy talent on many fronts simultaneously, while also maintaining a focus on common goals and higher purpose, even in the face of the ultimate challenge of war.

Perhaps most important, the Parthenon symbolizes the power of people reaching high-performance outcomes through a democratic process defined by the values of freedom and equality, by a conviction that citizens are their own masters, responsible for their own fate. Unlike the great pyramids of Egypt or the magnificent palaces of ancient Persia, the Parthenon was not built by an absolutist monarch to glorify his individual power. The Parthenon was erected by and for a company of citizens.

The decision to build it did not spring from the head of an egotistical tyrant; its construction was proposed by accountable leaders in an open forum, and a citizen assembly approved the work
plan. The project was led and staffed by highly skilled artisans,
but they were chosen and encouraged by the support of the
entire community that sponsored the project. Every step in the
process was carefully monitored by competent Athenian officials,
men who had been chosen for the task of oversight by their fellow citizens and who remained accountable to their fellow
citizens for the quality of the work. Public records made each
step in the building process transparent to any Athenian who
wanted to monitor the progress of the great enterprise that
would come to represent his organization to the world. Every
Athenian citizen, tens of thousands of people, contributed directly and indirectly to the completion of the project.

The Parthenon, with its grace, magnificent scale, and rich
refinement, proclaimed far and wide: This is what we Athenians
can do. This is who we are. We can do something like this because we are an enduring and wealthy community consisting of
tens of thousands of active, motivated, and participating citizens—each one a free and energetic individual. Our success is
not just a matter of our size, strength, and material resources;
even more important has been the contribution of our deep
store of knowledge and human capital, and our ability to innovate and perform with speed. We demonstrate that capability
through the exercise of our capacities as individuals and as citizens. Our values, our way of making decisions, and our ability
to work with one another allows us to do all this, and do it like
no other people in the world.

It is a very bold statement, but one amply justified by
history. The Parthenon was but one of many unprecedented

achievements of the ancient Athenian citizen community, the home of Sophocles, Plato, and Thucydides. In art, literature, drama, science, philosophy, naval technology, and military strategy, Athens became and remained an exemplar of innovation and cultural integration. In the year 431 B.C., the great Athenian statesman Pericles hauntingly forecast the enduring fame of his city's accomplishments:

> *Mighty indeed are the marks and monuments of our empire we have left. Future ages will wonder at us, as the present age wonders at us now. We do not need the praises of a Homer . . . for our adventurous spirit has forced an entry into every sea and every land; and everywhere we have left behind us memorials of good done to our friends or suffering inflicted on our enemies.*[4]

A product of tens of thousands of people working together to create something of lasting value and excellence, the Parthenon is the classic civic monument, a symbol of the world's first large-scale democracy—of Athens itself. It is a monument to people who thought, argued, voted, led, and followed, in a passionate quest for greatness, excellence, and justice. It represents people who faced life-and-death decisions together in the open air and on a common ground, who solved problems of politics, economy, and society through eloquent debate and who drove their city, through pain and jubilation, to some of the highest achievements of Western civilization. It also honors people who created a unique system to enable thousands to work together, to build great and beautiful things, to find new answers to age-old dilemmas, and to address a series of daunting challenges over a period of two centuries. And the Parthenon stands as a reminder to us that similar excellence can be achieved today.

THE MODERN PARADOX

The reemergence of democratic values, amid an ever-rising quest for high performance by organizations, reflects the most fundamental and urgent paradox of the knowledge economy today: How can leaders reconcile the idea of the organization as a sharply focused and aligned community with the idea of the organization as a mass of freedom-seeking, entrepreneurial individuals? This book presents a powerful and actionable solution, developed and time-tested by the world's first democracy. We will show how the performance value of a company of citizens results from its distinctive capacity to harmonize the goals of strong individuals within a cohesive organization.

As business globalizes and becomes ever more competitive, and customers and shareholders become ever more demanding, every firm must find ways to raise its performance by aligning and leveraging the collective skills and knowledge of its people. In brief, managers are faced with the question of "How can we learn to think and act as one?" The challenge is scaling human capability. Yet at the same time, there is another challenge: nurturing human individuality. Managers constantly seek to build people's capacity to "think differently"—they are tasked with fostering the creative freedom and personal autonomy of workers, who, in turn, expect to work in communities that respect the democratic values of freedom and equality. Within organizations we also witness a decline of hierarchy, the growth of flatter management structures, an increasing fragmentation and complexity of activity, and larger spans of management control. Meanwhile, knowledge workers are collaborating in teams, partnering across boundaries, and working more autonomously. Managers are combining employees, contractors, and suppliers in core processes while simultaneously holding them accountable within business or functional units.

Every manager confronts the following questions engendered by these simultaneously emerging trends: How do I scale, align, and focus ever-more-important human capability while also taking full advantage of the motivational power of individualism, entrepreneurial freedom, desire for equality, and the often unpredictable creativity required for innovation? How can I manage the complexity of decision making and governance of hundreds, even thousands, of knowledge workers bent on "doing their own thing"? Good managers cherish the engine of innovation that is created when talented people do their own thing— but how can they keep all that creativity aligned with a clearly articulated set of organizational goals? How can they distribute decision-making authority and responsibility widely, but not lose the focus on excellence? How can they let people participate in governance without sinking to the "lowest common denominator" of mob rule? In short: *How can they build community while building individuality at the same time?*

In creating their democratic city-state, the ancient Athenians faced each of these challenges, and many more. Their design and development of a civic system reflects innovative solutions that addressed the same basic paradox of individuality and community that confronts business leaders today. The citizen culture, with its values, structures, and practices, created an ethos of which each Athenian was proud to be a part. Their self-governing system encouraged unusually high commitment and alignment of every citizen, yet also encouraged a commitment to seeking the good of all. Decision making was knowledge-driven, participatory, and efficient. It balanced thoughtfulness and quick action and abhorred lowest-common-denominator solutions. Citizens were highly motivated and deeply engaged, combining personal purpose with commonly shared goals in the pursuit of excellence. Through civic institutions and interconnected networks, people learned how to leverage familiar trust-based relationships to build new working partnerships. The overall organization continually learned and constantly refined its knowledge. Leadership, embracing the values of citizen culture, reflected both the authority of individuals and their accountability to the community. In its civic design, Athenian culture was heterogeneous and homogeneous at the same time: open to the world and deeply proud of what was uniquely its own.

The individuality and community paradox appears in a completely different light when the organization *is* the people. In a citizen-centered company, people understand that they are themselves the ultimate means of production, with common values and common, performance-oriented goals. With the establishment of appropriate rights and responsibilities for people, and appropriate principles and processes of governance, a powerful and dynamic balance can be achieved between the alignment and focus of all members of the organization on the one hand, and freedom and equality among all individuals on the other. As we'll explain, the genius of this ancient habit of thought and action lies in its dynamic cultural system, built from three core elements: *democratic values, governance structures,* and *participatory practices*. This system reflects a continuous and interactive cycle of both "soft" and "hard" aspects of organization with powerful, self-reinforcing mechanisms that produce markedly high performance and innovation. In applying this system to our modern organizations, we have much to learn from understanding how the world's first "company of citizens" actually worked.

CREATING A COMPANY OF CITIZENS

The key to the success of the culture of the ancient Athenian company of citizens is a dynamic organizational model based on values, structures, and practices.

The Athenian concepts of *citizen, governance, democracy,* and *community* meant something very different to the Greeks than our contemporary notions of these terms. Removed from day-to-day decision making, most people's modern experience with constitutional government is distant and impersonal. Governing and political decision making are based on obscure rules and opaque practices, far removed from the lives of individual citizens. Modern citizenship still carries with it a sense of membership, but it is often a passive status focused on carrying a passport when you travel abroad, occasionally having an opportunity to vote for officials, or perhaps answering the summons to serve on a jury. Laws protect your rights against intrusions by the state, which is generally seen as a vast and impersonal corporate center. As citizens of a modern state, we admit that we need it to provide shared services (for example, national defense, local police, schools, and health care) and we fund it with our taxes, but we also assume that our ability to influence its direction is limited. Like many employees in large organizations, as citizens today we mostly seek to minimize the involvement of the decision-making bureaucracy in our daily lives. We know that as citizens in a modern democracy we are protected and maybe even supported in what we do to earn a living, raise a family, or pursue any kind of venture, but few would be likely to say that our major interests and concerns are intimately bound up with the legislative debates or legal decisions of our government.

That accommodating but distant—and perhaps even ironic—relationship between modern citizens and their government echoes the relationship between most employees and the firms they work in, a relationship caricatured (with an underlying truth, like all skillful caricatures) in the popular *Dilbert* comic strip. Only vaguely aligned, following rules and regulations as the path of least resistance, millions of Dilbert-style employees engage in a relatively passion-free contract with their company or organization, a contract based on a mutual exchange of goods and services. All too often, workers still find that they are being asked to check their values and sense of purpose at the door, just before punching the time clock. Not surprisingly, in most organizations, people's knowledge development and application, motivation, and performance are pale shadows of what they could be.

Ancient Athens was very different. Every person was actively engaged in learning and seeking a common purpose. Each participated with passion and commitment. The ancient Greek word for this form of citizenship—*politeia*—embraces a richness of meaning whose complexity is exactly the point—implying not just a passive legal status ("passport-carrying, tax-paying member of a nation"), but a deep and multifaceted sense of civic identity. The word *politeia* encompasses the concepts of "community of citizens," "constitution," "form of government," and even "way of life." At its core, *politeia* refers to a confluence of individual values with community values. The distinctive Athenian *politeia* was the alignment of those values with organizational structure, brought to life through practices of participation in the day-to-day work of governance. To be a member of the Athenian *politeia* meant that you thought, argued, and acted with your fellow citizens, and that you learned through the daily practice of civic life.

Politeia was simultaneously a concept, a social and political membership, a set of beliefs, and a set of behaviors that every day reinforced the integration of all those things together. In the democratic Athenian *politeia,* every citizen had the opportunity to participate in the governance of the organization, literally setting his own destiny: selecting and also serving as an official and engaging in all major decisions of the state. Each citizen also had the chance to serve, at least occasionally, as prosecutor, defender, and juror in trials of justice. Each had the chance to defend his community as a member of the armed forces. Through those community-building actions, the citizen saw the values of freedom and equality made real. He witnessed the commitments he made to his community, and those his community made to him, directly manifested in the structure of governance itself. Like the word "organization" for today's manager, *politeia* for the Athenian implied both intangibles and tangibles working together in a holistic system. With the holistic concept of *politeia* as a very special form of citizen-centered organization in mind, we can begin to unpack the main elements of the triad of values, structures, and practices that defined the culture of the Athenian company of citizens.

We begin with values because in today's knowledge age, the values that people bring with them when they come through the company door have more impact on organizational success than ever before. The Athenians placed importance on three core values: individuality, community, and moral reciprocity. Their notion of *individuality* was realized through the ideals of freedom, equality, and security: the right to live one's life as one pleased, to be ensured equal access to public privileges and responsibilities; and to be protected from physical or verbal assault or harm. The second value was the centrality of *community*—the belief that the citizens *are* the company. Athens, as an organization, was one and the same as the Athenian citizens themselves. There were influential Athenian leaders, but there was no abstract and remote "federal entity"—no government separate from the people. Nor was there a standing managerial class or ruling elite whose permanent role was to tell other people what to do. Every citizen's participation in governing the organization at the same time defined it, and leadership manifested itself as both ruling and being ruled. Because the citizen was the company, every individual was held accountable for decisions and for success or failure. Accountability was thus total and unambiguous, and the motivation to succeed was all-encompassing. The value of community served to moderate the value of individuality. Community values implied that the individual's freedom was the right to live one's life as one pleased, but only within the constraints of law and group norms. Equality and security were guarantees for each individual but they were not absolute; rather they were defined and made actionable by the community of which each person was a part. Personal freedoms were not protections against the group; they were embedded in the group itself.

The third core value, *moral reciprocity,* was based on the conviction that every citizen had a mission and duty to participate in promoting the common good of the organization, and by the same token the organization had a mission and duty to educate and fulfill each individual's full potential. This value further aligned the interests of the individual with the needs of the community. In exchange for commitment and devotion to the group, the individual could expect to be made better and grow. The process of self-governance was in a sense the agency of this development: Through each man's experience of acting, speaking, and leading in public affairs, he would become both a better individual *and* a more effective member of society. The individual citizen reciprocated the benefits he received as a member of the community by working to further the goals of his community. Such an approach was "reciprocal" because it offered a win-win proposition: The organization would grow and prosper with the growth and prospering of each individual as a fully participating member. It was "moral" because the reciprocal exchange of benefits between individuals and the community was carried out under conditions of justice, based on a shared conception of what constituted fair rules for the distribution of social and material goods.

Complementing these all-important but intangible values in the culture of citizenship were the very tangible structures of governance: institutions of decision making, justice, and managerial follow-through. As in modern systems, the governance structures of the ancient city-state included legislative assemblies, judicial bodies, and executive offices, along with the laws and established procedures to operate them and to uphold the processes of membership in the organization. But unlike modern governments, in democratic Athens all citizens were entitled, and indeed expected, to participate personally and directly in debate and decision making. In practice, a very large percentage of citizens did just that. They traveled long miles to the central city of Athens for the chance to talk, argue, and vote in an open assembly. They took turns steering the agenda as members of the citizen council and rotated leading functional offices as executives chosen by election or even by lot. They served willingly as members of huge juries, sitting in judgment on important matters of justice.

Our modern experience with systems of governance, along with standard textbook treatments of ancient Greek democracy, make it tempting to see the democratic institutions of classical

Athens as the defining dimension of citizenship. But putting these institutions first when seeking to understand the Athenian organizational model is a fundamental error. These structural institutions were not drivers, but rather outcomes of a new way of working; they emerged as artifacts and enablers of a distinctive culture, as a new habit of thought and action. Unlike most modern organization designs, the Athenian *politeia* did not start with a strategy, then devise a structure, and finally plug people into the framework. It began with the people themselves, and let values and structure and design emerge through the aligning practices of citizenship.[5] The result was sustained, dynamic performance. It remained dynamic over long periods of time, and through serious downturns, because the relationship between the intangibles and tangibles was organic and lively, with values fostering structure, and structure reinforcing and developing values through the medium of practice. The citizens' self-identification as citizens grew through their participation in democratic decision making. Over time, their own practical experience helped them develop better and more effective institutions of self-governance.

Practices of participation are the third element of the ancient citizenship model. These were the behaviors that determined how core values—individual, communal, and reciprocal—were manifested in social and institutional settings. Practices can be thought of as a set of marching orders that the citizens issued to themselves, exhortations by which they urged one another on to achieve great things: "Join in! Share what you know! Foster innovation! Take turns speaking!" But practices of participation were much more than cheerleading slogans. Just as the pragmatic manager describes organizational culture as "the way we do business around here," the Athenian citizen would articulate participatory practices as the "way we govern ourselves here in Athens," and they were intended as something that every citizen would learn and come to assimilate as his own. Practices keep abstract values in line with the concrete institutions of decision making, judgment, and execution. Practices are the mediation that brings the intangible and tangible together, that translates values into action. They define how people in the self-governing organization actually think and act. Practices are about both doing and learning from one another. They teach daily lessons about the meaning of citizenship and the role played by citizens in their democratic community. We discuss ten key practices that were prominent throughout the operations of Athenian democracy later in the book (see chapter 5). These ten practices gave life to the culture of citizenship in ancient Athens, and they provide a key to creating a company of citizens today.

LESSONS FROM HISTORY

Although the lessons of this book are based on a deep and detailed case study of an ancient city-state, we recognize that today's leaders are mostly concerned day to day with the economic dimensions of their companies. However, the challenges and discontinuities faced by the citizens of Athens will be hauntingly familiar: aligning and motivating people in the ongoing quest for higher performance; dealing with fierce rivals; balky allies and partners; year after year of constant conflict; shrinking of distances through new modes of transportation; breakdown of traditional social patterns and norms amid major commercial and trade revolutions; massive demographic changes; fundamental challenges to traditional forms of authority; and changing conceptions of the individual's place in the universe. For all their familiarity, the performance challenges that confronted ancient

citizens—questions of physical survival, the possibility of enslavement or total destruction—were orders of magnitude more
intense than the challenges today's managers confront when seeking to grow a business. The costs of failure in the ancient world—
including extinction of one's entire society—were greater than
any of the dangers faced by a modern business leader. We will
need to reflect on the significance of this "higher bar" in drawing insights from the case.

We must also disabuse readers of any notion that this case
presents a story of unmitigated success. Along with striking accomplishments, Athenian history also presents us with some
spectacular failures. And for all their wealth and glory in the classical age, the Athenians did not go on to conquer the world.
They lost their empire and eventually fell prey to rival world
powers, to the Macedonians (like Alexander the Great) and then
to the Romans. In our admiration for Athenian successes, we
must not forget that the Athenians failed to transcend certain aspects of their own historical context and unduly limited the scope
of applied justice and fairness: They never allowed women to be
citizens, acted brutally toward imperial subjects, and exploited foreigners as slave-laborers. These policies—to our modern eyes profound moral mistakes—had very practical consequences. Athens
never realized its true potential as a company of citizens because
it failed to extend its culture of self-governance far enough, and
thus succumbed to other powers. They failed to recognize the
value of women's participation[6] and denied citizenship to most
resident non-natives, imperial subjects, and slaves. And so they
denied themselves the expanded networks of human resources
and innovation that would have allowed them to better confront
their most dangerous opponents.[7]

With eyes open, we can acknowledge the limitations of this (or any) case study while also recognizing that Athenian failures will have their own lessons to teach. The differences between an ancient city and a modern firm can be turned into backhanded advantages when they are employed for the purpose of stimulating fresh thinking. For example, the extraordinarily high-bar performance challenges faced by ancient Athenians may prompt modern managers to consider the effects of intense pressure on the system and its ability to drive a self-governing organization to higher motivation and achievement. Let us also recognize that, whereas in the modern world "citizenship" has become primarily a political concept, the ancient Greek concept of *politeia* combined politics with society and economy—a blend of themes and issues increasingly appropriate to today's knowledge workers, who bring their whole selves to the workplace. Acknowledging the eventual demise of classical Athens, we should also recognize that its success and durability of some 200 years still places that organization near the top of all-time "built-to-last" rankings. How many global companies stay on the Fortune 500 list for more than a few decades? Two centuries of performance and resilience bespeaks a highly successful and sustainable system by any metric of organizational success today.

Rather than serving as an obstacle in the application of this case, the size of ancient Athens provides insights about the scalability of a self-governing organization. Contemporary examples of "workplace democracy" tend to be relatively small enterprises. With a population less than that of modern Luxembourg, Athens may look small when it is compared with modern nations. But compared with contemporary business organizations it is very large: The total population of classical Athens was some quarter of a million persons; of these at least thirty thousand were full citizens. The Athenian ability to structure and align a population of that size through a self-governing system shows that a high-performance balance of community and individuality can be scaled well beyond what managers today might imagine.

The modern business leader looking back on ancient Athens inevitably raises a related challenge—"What about technology?" Haven't telecommunications and the Internet fundamentally changed things—scale included? Indeed our global, electronically networked world today looks very different from preindustrial Mediterranean society. And no modern organization can fail to consider the value of computing and network technology in engaging and aligning its workforce. But as the wisest commentators and analysts have seen, the power of networks of people lies in *the people,* not the technology. The Athenian approach to networking so many highly individualistic people and creating processes of learning and working together on common projects can help us better understand that it is people who are the true source of a company's value. The case study of Athens allows managers to see more clearly the real essence of scaling knowledge work. Athens has much to teach today's leaders who worry about how to capture the advantages of intimacy as well as size, and who are concerned with keeping business units small enough to maintain agility while also operating within and across large extended enterprises.

In recent years, a steady stream of imaginative research has offered up new models for the "organization of the future." It has been compared to ecosystems, beehives, ant colonies, cloverleafs, medieval guilds, Hollywood film projects, jazz combos, and even chaotic systems of subatomic particles.[8] Each model makes important points. But few of them have really tried to understand the profoundly human processes that define human organization. Nor can they answer the difficult questions about sustainability and scale that arise as soon as people are treated as something other than cogs in a machine. We certainly learn something when we compare organizations to atomic particles or bees, but there is special value in a case study that focuses on people working over extended periods of time and solving the problems of governing thousands of individuals, each with human needs and aspirations. The philosopher Jean-Jacques Rousseau once asked whether "there can be any legitimate and sure principle of government, taking men as they are and laws as they might be."[9] This book takes today's knowledge workers just as they are: complex moral persons deeply committed to human values like equality and freedom. And it suggests a model for organizations as they actually might be: companies of citizens featuring self-governance structures in which freedom, equality, and other human values are made actionable in practice.

When Peter Drucker coined the term "knowledge workers" fifty years ago, he started us all on the path of understanding people-centered organizations—where "employees" become "professionals" and work not just with their hands but also with their heads.[10] But there is still much to learn. If human capability is becoming the key differentiator in the global economy, we must go beyond just thinking about heads and hands. People come to work not only with knowledge and skills, but with emotions and social needs.[11] The *Dilbert* comic strip reminds today's managers that motivating "knowledge assets" is a contradiction in terms. As every leader knows, organizing and motivating actual human beings is full of compromises and tensions. People are not mere tradable commodities; their potential and performance depend vitally on the organizational and social contexts in which they live. In today's competitive environment, motivating people (as opposed to "capital" or "assets") means paying attention to their deeper needs and human values. And this means that companies need to be something more than just internal markets for knowledge and talent.

The people who must be motivated are indeed the repositories of the knowledge and skills essential to a modern firm's success. But they also have concerns about identity and culture: about who they are and what they want to become.[12] They come through the door of their workplace caring about fairness and justice; they certainly don't want to be treated as either "knowledge assets" or "wage slaves." Not coincidentally, when the Athenians started their company of citizens, the first step they took was to forbid any Athenian from enslaving another Athenian. And thus they began the process of developing the world's first human-centric organization.

In today's global economy, harnessing the knowledge of people is critical, but the goal will never be accomplished unless the company pays real attention to people's innate desire to have a part in controlling their own destiny.[13] Managing today's firm cannot just be about managing knowledge. It must also be about people and their values, about human-centered governing structures, and about how values and structure are aligned by the daily practices of knowledge workers. Ancient Athens offers leaders a glimpse of what such a company might look like and the kind of performance it might achieve.

Any leader considering a new organizational case inevitably asks, "What does it mean for me? For my company? How can I apply it to my own situation?" Throughout this book we provide you with answers to those questions by offering specific ideas about how to develop a self-governing organization on the principles of ancient citizenship. We'll describe the role of performance objectives, building networks of networks, and the style of leadership appropriate to a citizen-style organization. These will, however, be general directions and implications rather than cookbook prescriptives. Our ambition is to introduce you to a habit of thought that will serve to inform rather than to define your own specific program of development. Leadership in the Athenian style is inspirational and can set bold new directions for an organization as a whole. Yet if the Athenian case teaches anything, it is that self-governance and the spirit of *politeia* is something that citizens must discover and develop largely through their own efforts. As the concept of democratic citizenship itself implies, building this kind of culture must be a process of "learning by doing" by the chief actors—the citizens themselves.

For leaders with the confidence to share power with their people, the lessons and design principles that emerge from the Athenian case are as timeless as the Parthenon itself. Although technology, economics, and global development will continue to evolve, when it comes to the fundamentals of people-centered organizations, the more things change, the more they will stay the same. The core building block of creating value will remain people working together for common goals. Success will accrue to organizations with the best strategy for enlarging, managing, and motivating a population of well-intentioned individuals. As long as human beings learn from one another in reasoned deliberation, as long as they become passionate when empowered with the chance to pursue goals they have defined for themselves, as long as free people reach for new heights of potential when treated as equals, the Athenian model will point to an approach to human organization that is both ancient and modern, noble and realistic.

CHAPTER 2

Citizenship in Action

THE YEAR IS 480 B.C. Dawn is breaking over the small Greek island of Salamis, just off the coast of Athens. Here, thousands of Athenian citizens are huddled on wooden ships, clutching weapons and oars, facing what seems like death itself. Across from them are hundreds of powerful warships, the majestic fighting navy of the Persian Empire. That force is poised to complete the Persian takeover of the Greek mainland, aimed particularly at the democratic city of Athens. Across the narrow strait, perched on a commanding hill, sits the Great King of Persia himself, eager to witness the culmination of years of preparation. He relishes the prospect of a historical and glorious victory.[1]

The Persian king's expectations were not based on foolish hopes. His empire had been expanding for the past seventy years; it had amassed huge capital resources and an equally huge array of armed forces. Persia was always on the lookout for new opportunities to grow, and Greece was now the obvious target. The Persian intelligence reports were encouraging: Greece was divided into hundreds of relatively small, fiercely independent city-organizations, given to frequent and costly fighting among themselves. In this year they had banded together to oppose the Persian invaders, but the alliance was fragile. A few months before, a Greek force that included 300 crack Spartan infantrymen had put up a surprisingly good fight in northern Greece, at the pass of Thermopylae. But superior numbers and a handy Greek traitor had turned the tide of the battle to the Persians. And now the king's navy was about to take on the outnumbered Athenians—the final obstacle blocking the domination of Greece. The Persian king expected no great difficulties. After all, the Athenians did not even have a monarch of their own to ensure that people obeyed orders.

Yet when dusk fell on that September day, the Persian king's grandiose plans were in ruins. An Athenian leader had developed a high-risk, high-payoff plan, squarely based on his fellow citizens' deep community orientation and their capacity to innovate. The bold plan had been carefully examined and quickly approved by the citizen Assembly. It was brilliantly carried out by Athenian executive officers. When it came to the fighting, the Athenians surprised, outmaneuvered, and outfought the Persian navy. Contrary to what the king and his generals assumed, the Athenians were not disorganized or in hiding. They were full of confidence in their own decisions and in their leadership. They trusted in the innovative battle plan they had agreed upon in the course of open deliberations. And as a result, their morale and indeed their performance were outstandingly high.

A newly built Athenian navy, a fleet of long, sleek, oared warships, whose construction had been mandated by the citizen Assembly, played the central role in the Greek victory over Persia.

The rowers who propelled the Athenian ships were not cowering slaves but proud and free citizens, who bent to their labor with discipline and determination. The Athenians made effective use of their special and collective knowledge of local wind conditions, and of the constricted geography of the narrow straits into which the Persians were lured. Their plan stymied the Persians despite their numerical advantage and threw their forces into confusion. With Persian momentum lost, heavily armed Greek soldiers jumped up from their posts on the Athenian boats and leaped from ship to ship, slaughtering the Persian crews. Survivors who swam to the island of Salamis were cut down by awaiting Athenian foot soldiers. The Greek underdog utterly routed the forces of the favored world power. Against all odds, a democratic fighting community had defeated a colossal monarchic military machine.

In the decades after their victory at Salamis, the Athenians proved quick to exploit the advantage and seized the new opportunities that their victory had opened up. During the fifth century B.C. the Athenians expanded their zone of influence across the Aegean Sea. Resiliently rebounding from setbacks and skillfully conjoining diplomacy with military might, they built the first great Greek overseas empire. The Athenian empire not only kept back the Persians, but also swept pirates from the sea, in the meanwhile collecting the equivalent of billions of dollars of taxes and tributes from an expanding universe of subject states. The Aegean became a safer place to trade. Commerce boomed, and many individuals, in Athens and in other Greek cities, benefited. Private and public wealth soared.[2]

At the same time, Athens hosted and spawned a cultural florescence the likes of which the world had never before seen. The atmosphere of the democratic city was open, experimental, and entrepreneurial—and at the same time results-oriented, with each person held accountable for his actions by the judgment of both markets and peers. Individual creativity was unleashed, and groundbreaking new ideas and practices emerged. Not only was the great Parthenon built, but many other masterpieces of architecture and sculpture were created. Athens became the place to be, and with its open society, philosophers, artists, scientists, and poets from across the Mediterranean world flocked to its academies, workshops, and public squares. Moral philosophy developed as a new discipline of thought, and the new art of writing history was developed by Herodotus and Thucydides. Drama became a great literary form with the production of tragedies by Aeschylus, Sophocles, and Euripides and comedies by Aristophanes. Scientists developed new theories ranging from the atomic structure of matter to the relationship of the earth to other heavenly bodies. This unprecedented cultural efflorescence, together with the accelerating rise of Athenian military power and technical acumen, resulted from a system of governance based on collective action and decision making and an open, democratic society.

The Athenians fought so well and so hard because they were seeking to defend their freedom, equality, and security (the values of individuality). They offered their lives in defense of their organization because they *were* the organization and because each man recognized that his own success was bound up in the collective success of Athens (the values of community). Their democratic governance structure allowed many people to contribute to the deliberations. The mutual trust that emerged through iterated practice allowed the Athenians to line up quickly behind a bold plan.

LEADERS AND FOLLOWERS

The plan that led to victory at Salamis in 480 B.C. was proposed to the Assembly of citizens by a dynamic leader named Themistocles. Among the most important elements of successful Athenian performance was the integration of inspired leadership and democratic decision making. Themistocles' leadership was an essential ingredient in the victory, and other leaders helped Athens to take over the Aegean and to build new markets in the decades that followed. Yet to understand *leadership* in the Athenian company of citizens we need to expand the modern conception of the term. The greatest Athenian leaders delicately balanced their individual vision and personal excellence with dedication to community orientation and collaboration. Leaders who failed to maintain the right balance could quickly lose their capacity to lead, and might find themselves dismissed. The career of Themistocles serves as an illustration.[3]

In the decade before the battle of Salamis, Themistocles had masterminded a plan to increase radically the size and capability of the Athenian navy. He recognized that Athenian democratic culture could easily support a much-enlarged navy, and he saw that a big navy could be the answer to defeating an expansionist Persia. Themistocles' battle plan for Salamis indeed made effective use of the new navy. Themistocles then played an important role in developing the Aegean network that soon became an Athenian empire. But Themistocles was far from the "CEO of Athens." He had no more authority than anyone else to order citizens around by managerial fiat. He held his position by being elected by his fellow citizens as one member of an important, but far from dominant, body of executive officers—the "Board of

Ten Generals." Themistocles, like other democratic leaders, had to win over his fellow citizens by persuasion and vision, not command and control. Like some insightful leaders of today's people-centered firms, Themistocles' greatness as a leader was solidly based on his ability to build engagement among people by clearly aligning their best interest with that of the organization overall. This is why his plan prevailed over the competing challenges of the many alternatives voiced in the Athenian Assembly.

Yet leadership in a company of citizens not only signified an ability to align people's interests with the interests of the organization, but also included a high level of personal accountability. After a series of remarkable successes, Themistocles allowed himself to forget that—with humiliating consequences. Over time, his increasingly egotistical, "uncitizenly" behavior led the Athenians to reject him as a leader. Within a few years after the battle of Salamis, he was officially "ostracized"—literally voted into a mandatory ten-year banishment from the city through a process in which the citizens cast votes on pottery shards (*ostraka*). Ostracism was one way the democracy got rid of leaders they found arrogant or otherwise bad for the city.

There were no golden parachutes for failed leaders in ancient Athens. Leadership of free citizens was a tough game, played by ambitious "honor-lovers" who knew that there were no safety nets. Anyone who thought enough of himself to take up public service also had to be ready to take real risks. The ostracism of Themistocles is part of an evolving pattern: The Athenian democracy relied upon strong and innovative leadership, but Athens as an organization never became dependent upon any one general or statesman. The citizens quickly dispensed with once-successful leaders who were no longer regarded as furthering the best interests of the community. Yet because the real power of decision making rested with the citizens themselves, and knowledge of how to govern the organization was widely distributed, changes in leadership did not necessarily mean a dramatic shift in direction for the city as a whole.

Leaders in Athens were not, however, just a disposable commodity. As we will see, great individuals left their stamp on Athenian policy. Leaders were important, and acknowledged as such. Those who proved successful were praised by their fellow citizens, and the memory of their great deeds was preserved for all time by contemporary monuments and historians. Leadership roles in this democratic governance system were crucial and well rewarded, although both roles and rewards were in some ways different from what leaders of most modern business organizations have come to expect. Yet in one crucial respect, Athenian leaders were very much like today's best leaders: They were responsible for helping to surface and focus the knowledge that lay dispersed throughout the organization.

Athenian leaders were deeply aware of the imperative of bringing to bear all the relevant knowledge held by many different people throughout the organization. But it was not their role to "manage" the knowledge of the citizens. A dynamic leader, like Themistocles, could and did add great value through his own distinctive vision. But that vision had to be, in each case, congruent with what the Athenian citizens collectively knew about themselves and what they knew about the challenges presented by the competitive environment in which they operated. No individual leader could claim to know more than what was known by "the entire people" about the organization as a whole. Nor could he hope to engage their followership without alignment between his vision and their willingness to execute a plan. Leadership was not a matter of telling Athenians what to do, but a matter of integrating what they already knew with a dynamic vision of new opportunities. The effective Athenian leader lined up the citizens' understanding of themselves as moral individuals with the particular challenge that faced them; and through artful and engaging language and communication he built the motivation of thousands around that vision.

Democratic leadership in the Athenian sense was never easy. It required a great capacity for communicating vision. Combine that communication challenge with "no parachutes" accountability, and you may well ask why anyone stepped up to the challenge. The answer is "love of honor." For Athenian leaders, deeply dedicated as they were to the ideals of freedom and equality, there was no higher honor than the esteem of free and equal people—their fellow citizens. They knew that the Persian king, for all his vast wealth and power, could never actually *earn* the respect of his followers. They realized that no hereditary ruler of lowly subjects ever enjoyed the satisfaction of knowing that he was being truly honored for his genuine qualities by his equals. Building a company of citizens offers leaders the chance— and also requires them—to gain the sincere respect and praise of people who are genuinely free and equal. In Athens, these intangible but valuable rewards of honor for leaders took the place of the disproportionate financial packages we see today—packages that can ultimately damage an organization's performance.[4]

The most successful and visionary of Athenian leaders in the imperial period after the victory at Salamis was Pericles.[5] Under his leadership, the Parthenon was built, and much of what the democracy of citizens achieved in this era bears the mark of his personal vision and organizational development skills. Yet Pericles was no autocrat. He saw clearly that Athenian greatness was a direct product of the public practices of the people themselves—

that the power of collective knowledge and collaborative engagement for the public good was an unstoppable strategy. He worked
through the Assembly of citizens to promote institutional
changes that served to make Athens more fully and effectively
democratic. Through Pericles' inspiring leadership, a more aggressive and wide-ranging reward structure—payment for public
service to Athens—was introduced; this encouraged Athenians at
all levels to devote even more of their time to furthering the good
of the organization as a whole.

In democratic Athens, it was not only the leaders who strove
to win honor. Everybody in the city-state, at some level, was engaged in the competition. Pericles and other leaders who helped
to build the democracy realized that for the system to work they
had to combine fair compensation with the more intangible rewards of seeing values in action, savoring victory, and gaining
public recognition. Moreover, Athens' democratic culture meant
that a leader did not have to start out life as a rich man. The governance structure provided leadership roles at many levels, and
even at the highest levels, through rotation and selection by lot.
Many relatively humble people took their turn leading major
decisions for the entire city-state.

The commitment to participation ran deep in the democratic
organization of Athens. It is estimated that, based on the average
citizen population of 30,000 and the number of officers needed
each year by the system, almost every citizen had the chance to
take a turn, at least once in his lifetime, at some substantial task of
public administration.[6] And that's above and beyond their military service, regular participation in open assembly several times a
month, and service on the huge jury courts that were characteristic of Athenian justice. This direct and participative democratic
system made the difference in Athens' performance.

RIVALS AND RESILIENCE

Athenian success in the era after the victory at Salamis bred imitators and competitors within the Greek world. Rival cities both envied the Athenians for their growing prosperity and feared them, wary of losing their own autonomy and traditional regional leadership positions. In southern Greece (the Peloponnesus) the historically great city of Sparta became increasingly apprehensive about the growth of Athenian power and wealth. The Spartans eventually realized that there was no limit to Athens' capacity to expand, a capacity that could eventually leave Sparta poor and isolated. Fearing such a fate, the Spartans declared war upon Athens in 431 B.C., just fifty years after the Greek victory at Salamis. The result was the long and devastating Peloponnesian War recorded by the historian Thucydides. It lasted for almost thirty years, ending finally in 404 B.C., with Athens' (temporary) defeat. It was a ruinous struggle, yet incredibly it ran in parallel with many of Athens' greatest cultural advances.

The Spartans were dangerous rivals indeed. Classical Sparta produced few enduring achievements of philosophy, sculpture, or literature, but the Spartans were, by any standard, highly competent experts in the arts of war. Spartan warriors were trained in military maneuvers from childhood; they lived in tight military brotherhoods and were feared for their single-minded dedication and skill at fighting Greek-style infantry battles. The elite Spartan shock-troops were supported on military campaigns by a much larger body of Greek soldiers, drawn from a Sparta-dominated partnership of cities in southern Greece (the Peloponnesian League). Unlike Athens, Sparta was not a democracy and refused to allow any of its partner cities to experiment with democracy as a form of government. Spartans favored central control and systematically opposed experimentation. It was a profoundly traditional society, but one that was also a major force to be reckoned with. When the Spartans and their allies marched into Athenian territory at the beginning of the Peloponnesian War in 431 B.C., most Greeks expected that Athens would soon fold—that the Athenians would be unable to maintain their far-flung empire and at the same time confront the Spartans in a major land war. Most believed that Athens would soon be forced to come to terms with Sparta, give up its imperial possessions, and so would soon return to the drab cultural level and limited productivity typical of a "normal" Greek city.

Such assessments failed to take into account the capacities of the democratic organization. Under Pericles' leadership, the Athenians put into practice an innovative war strategy, based on avoiding infantry battle with the Spartans, while maintaining control of the empire and guaranteeing vital imports by use of their navy. This unexpected strategy entailed giving up control of the Athenian countryside, where most Athenians had lived for generations. Just as when confronted with the Persian menace, the Athenians voted for a policy that entailed a very high level of individual sacrifice. The strategy worked for the Athenians for a long time, and there were many times in the course of the war that the Athenians could have made peace on very advantageous terms.

But the Athenians made several serious errors of judgment. Notably, after a six-year peace with Sparta, in 415 B.C., the Athenians, convinced that westward imperial expansion was a desirable goal, decided to attack another great Greek company of citizens: the city-state of Syracuse on Sicily. Conquering Syracuse was an overambitious performance objective, especially given that the Spartans were still strong and hostile and would be quick to exploit the opportunities opened as soon as their rivals over-reached. Misled by ambitious leaders and false information about the conditions they would encounter in Sicily, the Athenians seriously overestimated the capacity of their own democratic culture to overwhelm another city that was large, far distant, and well-supplied with local allies—and, by the way, also democratic in its governance. (We will examine other Athenian errors of judgment in subsequent chapters, showing how each can be traced to a failure to attend to the values, structure, and practices appropriate to a company of citizens.) The attack on Syracuse proved disastrous. The Spartans then allied with the "national enemy of Greece," Persia, and used Persian gold to build and man their own navy. After twenty-seven years of conflict, Athens finally lost the Peloponnesian War with Sparta. This heralded the end of the Athenian Empire and, temporarily, an end to democratic government at Athens.

Does the result of the Peloponnesian War refute the value of democratic governance and citizen-led culture? Through the ages, critics of democracy and advocates of Spartan-style command-and-control governance have pointed to this Athenian failure as proof that democracy does not work, claiming that it was the error-prone democratic decision-making process itself that led to Athens' fall.[7] But a deeper analysis suggests the opposite and also points to another critical characteristic of a company of citizens: the refusal to accept defeat as final, the persistence to keep going in the face of adversity, and the capacity to respond creatively and resiliently to a new environment. Accordingly, the critics' challenge prompts three important counterarguments.

First, we must remember that the Athenians held out against the Spartans for almost three decades. Second, the strength of the Athenian community was such that, even during this great war, it continued to develop and foster cultural innovations—while Sparta remained a grim and joyless military camp. Third, and perhaps most important, the success story of democratic Athens does not end with military loss to the Spartans in 404 B.C. In the decades after 404, Athens rebounded economically and the democracy and cultural vitality of Athens continued for another century or more. Meanwhile, Sparta declined to insignificance within a generation of its hard-won military victory. It's an important lesson of history that the winner doesn't always take all. Through the darkest times, the Athenians endured and insisted on continuing their democratic culture. Truly successful organizations are capable of achieving great results, but they must also be capable of surviving serious setbacks.

After the war, the Spartans sought to control Athens by abolishing democracy and imposing a hierarchical pro-Spartan system of governance. The new puppet leaders proved greedy and brutal, stripping away key Athenian assets, driving talented people out of the city, and perverting the governmental system toward a factionalism that ended up implicating others in their murderous schemes—including the famous Athenian philosopher, Socrates. But the democratic spirit proved resilient in the face of catastrophe. In the year 404 B.C., patriotic Athenians, driven from the city, prepared to take back control of their organization. First seizing a small outpost in the Athenian hinterlands, they attracted a growing body of fighters and financial backers to their side. With a large assembly of well-armed supporters, including citizens, foreigners, and even slaves, the democrats soon recaptured the city from the Spartan puppet government.

Following their repossession of Athens, the democratic citizens set about the tough process of rebuilding their city, a process that required bold new thinking. Realizing that any attempt to recreate their lost empire must fail in the staunchly anti-imperialist postwar Greek environment, they turned the crisis of losing a great war into an opportunity. The Athenians changed their strategy nimbly; turning away from their prewar focus on imperial conquest, they began to build new wealth by focusing on their own resources and skills. More efficient exploitation of Athenian silver mines and other local products provided a new capital base. Meanwhile, by developing its excellent ports and open, entrepreneurial culture, Athens quickly regained its place as the center of Aegean trade. The Athenian legal system was streamlined to better accommodate the concerns of traders and financiers resident in the city. Foreigners with capital to invest returned to Athens, and the city prospered. A new generation of leaders stepped forward to guide the Athenians in pursuing this new strategy, but the ultimate source of renewed performance was the Athenian ability to surface and draw upon fresh ideas and original contributions from a diverse population of citizens. Once again, in periods of recovery as in periods of expansion, the Athenian case shows that thoughtful leadership is essential, but also underlines that in a challenging environment the successful leaders of a company of citizens will focus on tapping the key resource of a citizen-centered organization: the power of collective energy and enterprise.

One of the newcomers to the city of Athens was a slave named Pasion. In many ways, he symbolizes the postwar era, the second great age of Athenian democracy. Pasion worked for the owners of a prominent Athenian bank. The entrepreneurial spirit of the city had encouraged the development of new instruments of credit, allowing for more effective leveraging of capital. Pasion, who proved to be a master financier, adept at managing the very high-risk business of making loans to Athens-based overseas traders, was at the center of this development. He eventually made enough money for his masters that he was able first to purchase his own freedom and then to take over the active management of the bank. In the process, Pasion became very rich. He knew that slavery was endemic to the Mediterranean world, yet Athens offered a man with his talents the chance to prosper. Consequently, he was also deeply loyal and financially generous to the city that had fostered the environment in which he was able to come so far. The citizens reciprocated his public generosity with the grant of the greatest gift they could offer: Athenian citizenship for Pasion and his sons. Pasion's eldest son went on to become a prominent democratic leader in later years. Even while retaining the morally indefensible practice of enslaving foreigners, Athenians also encouraged an unprecedented openness to upward mobility.[8]

The city as a whole benefited enormously from the entrepreneurial talent of men like Pasion. Thanks to them, the volume of Athenian trade increased dramatically in the course of the fourth century B.C., and with it grew Athens' public and private wealth. Commercial gain and the tax revenue it generated came to replace the public and private wealth that had been created by the former Athenian empire. The great navy was built anew, eventually surpassing the size of the fifth-century fleet. But the Athenian navy was now used primarily to support commercial rather than imperial purposes—to protect key trade routes. Meanwhile, Athens remained a center of intellectual and cultural innovation. Philosophy flourished as Plato and Aristotle opened their famous schools in Athenian suburbs. Technical treatises were published on mathematics, music, science, household management, state finances, and medicine. Athenian writers experimented with new literary genres, creating the first autobiography and the first historical novel of Western civilization. The art of public speech reached new heights with orators like Demosthenes and Aeschines, and Athenian art broke new ground with the works of Praxiteles and other sculptors. Athens' power, prosperity, and cultural vibrancy reemerged, and its dramatic recovery from the brink of destruction must be directly attributed to the values, structures, and practices of participatory democratic culture.

THE INSIDERS' VIEW

Athens' long-term success was based on a pioneering and unusually effective approach to organization: it was an approach that leveraged the collective knowledge of a large and diverse population, and one that, through broad-based empowerment, cultural values, and continuous learning, consistently motivated people to work hard and to fulfill clearly articulated goals. The key to Athens' success was a breakthrough in ideas about governance by citizens: It is no accident that the same city that came to dominate the Aegean and created much of the basis of Western culture also invented a new system of citizen-based self-rule. Democratic governance was the engine that drove Athenian performance, brought Athens to the heights of power and prosperity, and allowed Athens to recover from seemingly catastrophic reverses.

The connection between democratic culture and outstanding performance is clear in hindsight. But the ancient Greeks themselves also recognized that connection and wrote eloquently about it. One of the most famous descriptions of Athenian citizen-culture and democracy was spoken (according to the historian Thucydides) in Sparta by diplomats from the city of Corinth, on the eve of the great Peloponnesian War. The Corinthians, rivals of the Athenians and allies of Sparta, sought to explain the essential nature of their foes' democratic organization. The speech clearly had a political purpose—to fan the fires of war against the Athenians. But beneath the rhetorical flourishes lay a shrewd analysis.

The year is 431 B.C. and the scene, set for us by Thucydides, is the assembly of the Spartan leaders. The Corinthian ambassadors are making their pitch to have the Spartans join them in war against the Athenians. In so doing, they describe what kind of people the Athenians really are, contrasting them to the more conservative and slow-moving Spartans:

> *An Athenian is always an innovator, quick to form a resolution and quick to carry it out . . . Athenian daring will outrun its own resources; they will take risks against their better judgment, and still, in the midst of danger, remain confident . . . While you [Spartans] are hanging back, they never hesitate; while you stay at home, they are always abroad; for they think that the farther they go, the more they will get . . . If they win a victory, they follow it up at once, and if they suffer a defeat, they scarcely fall back at all . . . They regard [their bodies] as expendable for their city's sake, as though they were not their own; but each man cultivates his own intelligence, again with a view to doing something notable for his city. If they aim at something and do not get it, they think that they have been deprived of what belonged to them already; whereas, if their enterprise is successful, they regard that success as nothing compared to what they will do next . . . If they fail in some undertaking, they make good the loss immediately by setting other hopes in some other direction. Of them alone, it may be said that they possess a thing almost as soon as they have begun to desire it, so quickly with them does action follow upon decision . . . Their view of a holiday is to do what needs doing; they prefer hardship and activity to peace and quiet.[9]*

The Corinthian ambassadors described the Athenians as rest-less and nimble entrepreneurs, bound together for collective suc-cess. It is a vision of democratic performance told from the point of view of a traditional, hierarchical organization—one that was profoundly unsettled by the growing success of Athens. As in many modern organizations, the entrenched leadership of a traditional enterprise looked on the bold upstart's initiative with a combina-tion of awe and apprehension. Democracy was something new on the Greek scene, and the Corinthian leaders realized, quite rightly, that the Athenian approach was a threat to all traditional Greek city-organizations. The traditional cities would be forced to change or find themselves losing their competitive edge.

At the end of the speech to the Spartans, the Corinthians warn of superior Athenian innovation, and the timeless necessity of confronting and adapting to change:

> *[Y]our whole [Spartan] way of life is out of date when compared with theirs. And it is just as true in politics as it is in any art or craft: new methods must drive out old ones. When a city can live in peace and quiet, no doubt the old-established ways are best; but when one is constantly being faced by new problems, one has also to be capable of approaching them in an original way. Thus Athens, because of the very variety of her experience, is a far more modern state than you.*[10]

Some 2,400 years ago, the Corinthians argued to their allies that constant change demanded constant innovation. They saw clearly that the city-state that had figured out how to do that was Athens and its culture of entrepreneurial, self-governing citizens.

If the Corinthians offered a rival's view of the Athenian com-pany of citizens, the Athenians' own leader, Pericles, provided a more favorable but still consistent picture of the same phenom-enon. Pericles sought to define for his fellow citizens the source of Athenian greatness in a now legendary speech (again, reported by Thucydides). His public "Funeral Oration," commemorating the sacrifice of Athenian soldiers in the war with Sparta in 431 B.C., captured the soul and spirit of the company of citizens. It pinpointed the very essence of democratic culture—the combination of values, structure, and practices that characterized the Athenian culture of governance.[11]

In his speech, Pericles starts by stating that his goal is to discuss the values and practices that allowed the Athenians to build a powerful empire and face a series of crises and setbacks. He states bluntly that it is "our citizenship (*politeia*) and way of life which has made us great," and he immediately identifies democracy as the key factor in Athenian success. He points out that Athenian-style democracy leads to innovative meritocracy, where genuine individual ability rather than inherited position or status is the key to advancement in the organization:

> *Our constitution is called a democracy because power is in the hands not of a minority but of the whole people. When it is a question of settling private disputes, everyone is equal before the law; when it is a question of putting one person before another in positions of public responsibility, what counts is not membership in a particular class, but the actual ability which the man possesses. No one, so long as he has it in him to be of service to the state, is kept in political obscurity because of poverty. And, just as our political life is free and open, so is our day-to-day life in our relations with each other. We do not get into a dispute with our next-door neighbor if he enjoys himself in his own way . . . We are free and tolerant in our private lives; but in public affairs we keep to the law.*

Moreover, says Pericles, Athens is characterized by complete openness in respect to knowledge, talent, and new ideas. While recognizing that Athens' enemies may occasionally benefit from this openness, Pericles is convinced that the Athenians themselves gain much more from their own brand of freedom and liberality:

> *Our city is open to the world, and we have no periodical deporta-*
> *tions in order to prevent people observing or finding our secrets which*
> *might be of military advantage to the enemy. This is because we rely,*
> *not on secret weapons, but on our own real courage and loyalty. There*
> *is a difference too in our educational systems. The Spartans, from*
> *their earliest boyhood, are submitted to the most laborious training*
> *in courage; we pass our lives without all these restrictions, and yet we*
> *are just as ready to face the same dangers as they are.*

Pericles was doing more than just contrasting Spartan discipline with raw Athenian talent. His point was that Athenian talent was deeply grounded in democratic culture—it was a community whose values and ways of working brought the best out of people.

Throughout the speech, Pericles explores Athens' democratic culture. He points to his fellow Athenians' embrace of paradox: the balance of individual freedom with public commitment, openness to the world combined with intense loyalty for community, respect for advance planning but also intense bias for action. Embracing paradox is indeed the challenge for a modern organization in the Knowledge Age: concern for people, but also concern for performance; having strong values, but also being open to change; thinking globally while also acting locally. This sort of "both/and" thinking permeates Pericles' vision of Athenian citizenship.[12] In a famous passage of the speech, he paints a picture of an organization that is one and the same as its people; its subtle interplay of private rights and public concerns; and the sublime balance Athenians are able to strike among what are often seen as polar opposites:

Our love of what is beautiful does not lead to extravagance; our love of the things of the mind does not make us soft. We regard wealth as something to be properly used, rather than as something to boast about. As for poverty, no one need be ashamed to admit it: the real shame is not taking practical measures to escape from it. Here each individual is interested not only in his own affairs but in the affairs of the city as well . . . We do not say that a man who takes no interest in politics minds his own business; we say that he has no business here at all. We Athenians . . . take our decisions on policy or submit them to proper discussions: for we do not think there is an incompatibility between words and deeds . . . We are capable at the same time of taking risks and estimating them beforehand . . . We make friends by doing good to others, not by receiving good from them. This makes our friendship all the more reliable . . . When we do kindnesses to others, we do not do them out of any calculations of profit or loss: we do them without afterthought, relying on our free liberality.

Toward the end of the speech, Pericles compares Athens to a school—with a citizenship and way of life which serves to develop each of its members as a unique and gifted individual.

Taking everything together then, I declare that our city is an education to Greece, and I declare that in my opinion each single one of our citizens, in all the manifold aspects of life, is able to show himself the rightful lord and owner of his own person, and do this, moreover, with exceptional grace and exceptional versatility.

Although he could not have known that 2,400 years later business leaders might be reading his words, Pericles knew he was speaking about something of real significance and lasting value. The proof of the accuracy of Pericles' description was the Athenian company of citizens in action.

KNOWLEDGE AND PERFORMANCE

Within a year of Pericles' great speech in 431 B.C., the Athenians, now engaged in the great Peloponnesian War, were fighting on multiple fronts with the Spartans. Adding to the pressure, a devastating plague descended on the city, an unknown disease that raced through the population and had soon killed at least one of every four Athenians. As human and capital resources were stretched thin, the company of citizens challenged their field commanders to gain "smart" victories, using whatever men and ships they had to maximum effect against the Spartans. One commander was an Athenian admiral named Phormio who was leading a modest fleet of twenty oared warships stationed at the Athenian-controlled port city of Naupactus (in the Corinthian Gulf, to the west of Athens). Phormio's mission was to stop a much larger enemy fleet of Spartan allies from moving west out of the Gulf, and to prevent their land-sea attack on Athenian allies in northwestern Greece. His story offers clear lessons about citizenship in action.[13]

Phormio's strategy began with a surprise attack, startling the enemy, who had not imagined that the small Athenian force would dare challenge them. In fact, so sure were the Spartan allies of their passage that they had loaded their warships with armored infantrymen, which weighed them down. Phormio plunged ahead against his stunned enemy. At first the Peloponnesians tried to shake off the Athenians, but the latter were too swift. The enemy thus drew up in defensive position, deploying their ships in a large circle with their ramming prows facing outward. Phormio advanced boldly, the Athenian ships rowing in close order round and round their opponents, periodically feinting toward the enemy in simulated attacks. Phormio's clever tactics fooled the disconcerted opposing commanders. They further constricted their defensive circle of ships, and that left them with less and less room in which to maneuver. When, as Phormio had anticipated, the strong morning wind came up and buffeted their ships, the Peloponnesian warships were caught off guard and fell into confusion. The Athenians attacked in earnest, sinking one of the commanders' ships and disabling others. The remaining ships broke ranks and fled. The Athenians pursued, capturing twelve vessels, and returned with their prizes back to Naupactus.

The Spartans back home were furious and humiliated upon hearing the news of the defeat. They immediately dispatched new officers along with reinforcements to their fleet, mandating a return attack. As the new battle began, Phormio was forced by the enemy's superior numbers to sail into shallow and constricted waters, and he soon lost nine of his twenty ships. The Spartan commanders set off to pursue the surviving eleven Athenian ships, but ten of them made it safely to the harbor of Naupactus. The eleventh Athenian ship, closely pursued by a Peloponnesian warship, then performed a shocking maneuver. Sailing right around a merchant ship that happened to be anchored outside the harbor, the Athenian ship gained the key prow-on advantage, rammed into the side of the pursuing Peloponnesian warship, and sunk her. The crews of the other Spartan ships, who witnessed this sudden reversal, were again stunned. Taking advantage of the confusion, the ten Athenian ships in Naupactus harbor then charged out. Momentum and timing gave them an easy victory: the outnumbered Athenians captured six enemy ships, and recovered all nine ships that had been taken by the Spartans in the first part of the engagement. The remainder of the Spartan fleet withdrew in terror.

This story illustrates Phormio's savvy leadership, but it is also a tale of the organizational capability of a company of citizens. The Athenian victory reflects their navy's superior technical prowess and ability to execute complicated tactical maneuvers that other Greeks simply couldn't do. The Athenians had better ships and also better oarsmen. One hundred and seventy rowers propelled each massive warship, a task that required both precision and discipline. The Athenian rowers were not just a bunch of strong backs; they were talented knowledge workers in their own right. The practices of citizenship encouraged agile and innovative fighting; they allowed Athenians to do more with less.

Ramming and some of the other specialized naval tactics employed by the Athenians required high levels of training, as well as split-second, real-time coordination for rowers and helmsmen alike. Athenian crews operated as highly skilled, nonhierarchical teams. Their organization and tactics also limited casualties much more than the traditional "grapple and board" approach typical of the Spartans, who were much readier to lose rowers as expendable "assets." Minimizing casualties and manning ships as teams of fellow citizens reflected a mind-set of the Athenian democratic culture: work smarter and quicker, respect and learn from your fellow citizens, and use intelligence instead of brute force to win. The elected Athenian commanders—themselves citizens—trusted the rowers to do their job well; and the rowers in turn trusted their commanders to execute bold maneuvers— minimizing the risk of their own deaths.[14]

The practical knowledge that made possible Phormio's victory at Naupactus was widely distributed among the citizens who dominated the Athenian war forces. Phormio, as a leader, deserves much credit for the victory, but his strategic insight was not the only factor of success. The audacious maneuver on the spur of the moment by the anonymous commander of the "eleventh ship," and the astonishing skill of its oarsmen and helmsman, tell us that high-level capabilities and cleverness were expected of all Athenian naval personnel. Moreover, Athenian ships themselves embodied the ideals of democratic culture. They were lighter and faster than those of other Greeks, and we know that they were developed, through iterative innovations in previous years, in tandem with the development of specialized training and rowing techniques—by citizens, working together in teams, and spirited by the values of *politeia*. Athenian naval technology was constantly being developed and improved, through an ongoing exchange of knowledge, techniques, innovations, and new practices among Athenian rowers, helmsmen, naval architects, shipwrights, field commanders, and generals. As Pericles said in his speech, Athens' open and democratic culture fostered continuous learning and improvement.

Athenian citizens were genuine knowledge workers, and they flourished under a system of values, institutions, and practices of democratic citizenship. Their creative advances and continuous improvement can also be seen in the development of their cavalry, marines, construction crews, and home-guard infantry. Democratic culture encouraged citizens to apply what was learned in one sphere of activity to another, encouraging more active learning and actionable application. Citizens easily "cross-appropriated" what they learned between their military and civic services: their experience as participatory citizens made them more effective warriors, and their experience of military discipline made them more effective decision makers.[15] Driven by common purpose, the citizens working together created a systematic exchange of learning among designers and builders of ships, the citizens rowing them, the citizens steering them, the generals deploying them, and even the citizens sitting in the

Assembly deliberating over whether to authorize more money to build more of them. The culture was marked by everyone having a chance to speak, to vote, and to decide—all taking turns in both administering things and serving in the army or navy itself. Accountability and performance challenge went hand in hand— in war, remember, the very survival of the community was on the line in each contest. Success was celebrated with honor, but missteps and failures were punished by the community—indeed, Phormio himself later faced trial for misuse of public funds.

The Naupactus campaign also reflects the importance of Athenian values of individuality—equality, freedom, and security—to Athenian military performance. The city celebrated the basic equality of all Athenians, and as Pericles said, their democracy was based on the belief that each citizen had the capacity to join with his fellows in judging how best to keep the city secure. The Athenian concept of freedom implied an equal right for all to open and unfettered speech. These values were made real in participatory practices like engagement, merit, deliberation, and transparency. The result was a community in which everyone expected that any colleague who possessed special knowledge pertaining to the common good would present what he knew to the relevant parties; and similarly that any colleague who had such knowledge would come forward in support of the greater good of the community. The citizens saw that participating in such exchanges and mutual self-improvement would improve each individual and help secure the city in time of war. Because of their continuous practice of speaking and learning from one another in the structural institutions of the democracy, they were well schooled in how to do so. This sort of free-flowing exchange of knowledge is encouraged in many progressive modern firms.[16] But the Athenians exchanged knowledge on a vastly larger scale—among tens of thousands of people, and without the aid of modern technology.

How did it all work in practice? As a background to Phormio's victory at Naupactus we must imagine an array of practical knowledge exchanges: a veteran rower passing along tips and techniques to his younger benchmate; helmsmen collaborating on ramming tactics; shipwrights speaking up at a discussion of the financing of new ship building in the Assembly. The participatory culture had at its foundation the sense of the individual taking responsibility for both himself and the community overall—not just bravely sacrificing oneself in battle, but also freely offering one's knowledge and experience in public and for public benefit. As the Corinthians had said: "[T]hey regard [their bodies] as expendable for their city's sake, as though they were not their own; but each man cultivates his own intelligence, again with a view to doing something notable for his city."

A fundamental lesson of Athenian performance is that democratic culture does not require that everything be dragged down to the lowest common denominator or demand bland conformity. Athenian habits of citizenship fostered the practice of debating the merits of many new ideas, everyone having a say in the final outcome, and everyone taking collective responsibility for the implementation of the best possible decisions. At the same time, the Athenians were famously individualistic. The Athenian's freedom to choose his lifestyle was often contrasted with the Spartans, who submerged their individuality beneath an ideal of "uniformity." Essential to Athenian agility was the versatility of the individual upheld in tandem with the cooperative habit of working in teams with others. The Athenian warrior—whether infantryman or oarsman—possessed a variety of skills, and the capacity to shape and adapt his skill-set in unfamiliar conditions.

But as many campaigns in the long war with Sparta showed, he also knew how to form teams, build networks, and improvise tools and strategies as required.

Another lesson of democratic performance is the importance of "both/and" thinking. Through their participation in the democratic culture of the city, Athenians learned both to "think alike" and to "think differently." An innovative leader's "different-thinking" plan always depended upon a large body of Athenians recognizing the value of the new idea, and actively backing it by forming teams and lending their minds and bodies willingly to the new enterprise. But the success of "different-thinking" plans also required a high level of consensus. Once discussion had been concluded and the vote taken, the Athenians willingly joined forces behind the successful proposal. Putting the debate behind them, they acted cohesively in teams that "thought alike" in recognizing and working toward the agreed-upon goal. It was the genius of the democratic organization to be able to bring groups of unique individuals together, to leverage the diverse knowledge possessed by very different people, to use that knowledge as the basis of participatory decision making, and then to unite the entire organization behind the plan of action. Combining "thinking differently" and "thinking alike" did not guarantee success in every enterprise, but it allowed the Athenians to learn from, and rebound from, even their most serious failures.

In sum, as a direct result of their democratic culture—their union of values and structures through participatory practices—Athenian-style citizen performance was characterized by:

Community orientation: The willingness to sacrifice, voluntarily, narrow private interests for the public good, while still encouraging the highest pursuit of individual

excellence, defines the relationship of individual to community. The citizen is always asking how he can do
something good for the community, with the reciprocal
expectation that when the community prospers, so
will he.

Openness: The community allows for the coming and
going of others, liberally ready to embrace talent and
ideas from anywhere. The Athenians saw that the risk of
"stolen secrets" was outweighed by the power of access-
ing fresh thinking and influences from others, as well as
openly sharing knowledge among themselves.

Responsive leadership: Leaders remain citizens, responsible to their company of citizens. They take on authority
through rotation; as Aristotle famously said, each member of the community is able "both to rule and be ruled,
taking turns." Citizen leaders work with the entire organization to surface new ideas and shape collective action. And they remain accountable to the judgment of
their fellow citizens.

Innovation: Citizens are always increasing their capacity
for new ideas and building on each technical advance
they made—whatever the arena—with more experiments and successes. So they're always one step ahead
of their competitors.

Time-sensitivity: Citizens consistently move faster than
their rivals. They seamlessly combine new thinking with
open discussion and discussion with bold action, and so
they work smarter and faster all the time. Democracy is
not opposed to speed; it thrives on it.

Entrepreneurial spirit: A company of citizens is always
out looking for more, using creative insight and energy
to exploit opportunities. They don't just "stay at home,"
and they don't settle for what they have. They want to
expand and are willing to take risks. This entrepreneurial
spirit is embodied in the entire community, and reinforced by practices of citizens working together.

Resilience: Citizens refuse to be discouraged by setbacks,
even terrible ones, like defeat in a war. They rebound
and come back for more. In this they are like the greatest
companies that endure, year in, year out, even during
downturns. They are insistent on achieving success and
resilient in the face of failures.

Agility: Citizens are flexible and change-ready. Their organization can shift direction quickly and adapt itself dynamically to new circumstances. Their success is built
not simply on strength but on nimbleness, "thinking on
the fly," and adapting readily to new conditions.

Athenian military and commercial performance, both in its
successes and its failures, offers many lessons for building today's
company of citizens. First, although a democratic-style governance culture is no guarantee of high performance, the Athenian
case demonstrates that with the right system of values, institutions, and practices—and indeed one that maximizes collective
knowledge and human potential—astonishing things can be
achieved. Second, there can be no doubt about the importance of
aligning such a culture with specific performance objectives—
steep, even life-threatening challenges do wonders for forcing
a balance between the power of pluralism and the necessity of

focused action. Third, a key metric of organizational success, especially for such a culture, is not just "winning" but "winning and coming back from defeat." A culture of citizens will necessarily make mistakes along the way—indeed such is the price of innovation and collective engagement—but if the culture's values, institutions, and practices are deeply integrated, and leaders give people true responsibility for their own destiny, the organization can show amazing resilience.

The power of the Athenian organization—to be simultaneously committed to individuality and to community—is an inspiring model for any Knowledge Age organization wrestling, as all inevitably do, with that paradox of managing and scaling human capability. In the next chapter we'll look back to the original invention of citizenship at Athens. Where did the values, institutions, and practices come from? How did they evolve into an integrated system and culture that created the unprecedented achievements of this ancient, preindustrial city-state?

CHAPTER 3

The Invention of Citizenship

THE INVENTION of democratic-style citizenship ranks among the greatest accomplishments of Greek civilization. Indeed, it is arguably among the greatest of all human inventions, comparable to the invention of the alphabet, the corporation, or computer software. Like these other advances of civilization, citizenship required inventors; it was not a naturally occurring entity just waiting to be discovered and employed by a thoughtful leader. Citizenship is a remarkable *technology of self-governance*. It was developed in response to the demands posed by the hypercompetitive environment of the rivalrous Greek city-states and the intense pressure to develop a new form of human organization that could thrive within that environment. The invention did not take place all at once, but in a series of revolutionary and evolutionary stages.[1] At each stage we witness how both leaders and followers developed an intelligent organizational response to challenge and sought both to capture new opportunities for the members of the community and to avert loss and destruction at the hands of enemies. The company of citizens emerged in the crucible of great rewards and great dangers, both external and internal.

Two centuries before the Parthenon was built, in the seventh century B.C., families of contentious local warlords dominated Athens. These strongmen worked together, governing Athens as an oligarchy of powerful land-owning families. But toward the end of the seventh century the first of a series of revolutionary events dramatically changed the nature of the community: One of the warlords sought to seize control of the entire territory of the Athenians and thus establish himself as tyrant over all. This resulted in the first recorded uprising of Athenians in defense of their existing form of governance against the threat of an absolute ruler, and the would-be tyrant was put down. In addition, many of his supporters were slaughtered, despite the ruling families' promise of amnesty. In the aftermath of the failed coup and its bloody denouement, the Athenian warlords saw that their society was headed for more strife unless major changes were made. In an effort to stabilize the situation, they adopted the first-ever Athenian written code of homicide laws, which set the rules regulating revenge killing. But the social and political climate remained volatile. A few years later, there was a renewed threat of civil war, fired by economic change and the social distress caused by the growth of the practice of enslaving local people who had fallen into debt and the exploitation of struggling Athenians by the wealthy landowners. Amidst the renewed crisis, in the year 594 B.C., a visionary leader emerged, gaining fame through public performances of patriotic poetry. Fearing that they would lose everything if a civil war broke out, the warlords appointed him magistrate with extraordinary law-making powers. His name was Solon.

Solon recognized that society would never be stabilized unless the power of the wealthy few was counterbalanced by the guarantee of legal immunities that would protect all Athenians against unjust practices. He solved some of the most pressing problems of his people by implementing a series of bold and innovative reforms. He ended servitude based on debt, and even more important, he abolished the practice of one Athenian enslaving another. Until that time, powerful Athenians really could treat their weaker neighbors as "fungible assets"—people could be bought and sold just like any other sort of goods. After Solon's reforms, enshrined in a code of law that all Athenians swore to uphold, all Athenians were forbidden to enslave their countrymen. Now "Athenian" signified much more than "someone who happens to live in Athenian territory"; it meant "someone who cannot be owned by another Athenian." With this simple but powerful change, they began the process of inventing citizenship.

Solon also established a more sophisticated civic government, implementing a process that allocated executive offices and public duties to individuals according to their wealth, rather than (as before) their aristocratic ancestry. The new system was based on a calculation of annual personal income. Although this was still far from complete equality of opportunity, it was a creative and brave move toward the recognition that service to the community should be based on some level of accomplishment—merit, judged by financial success—rather than family heritage. In a more explicitly democratic reform, Solon also established the institution of a governing citizen assembly, open to all adult male Athenians, and he confirmed the people's power of authorizing any major decision that affected the whole community.

Like Winston Churchill, Solon was both a great statesman and an inspiring writer. Solon's autobiographical poetry shows that he intentionally precipitated a revolution based on innovative, people-centered ideas. About his own accomplishments Solon writes:

Many who had been sold abroad I brought home
To divinely-wrought Athens . . .
And others too, who had fled
From dire constraint of need, people who even
Forgot their native tongue, so widely had they wandered.
And others suffering humiliating slavery
Right here at home, trembling before their masters' anger,
I set them free. These deeds I made prevail.
Aligning power with justice, so they fit together,
I accomplished just what I had promised.
And I drafted equal rules of law for people of different rank,
Fitting straight justice to each man's case.[2]

In these verses, we see the process of *politeia*-building in action. Solon was creating an organization that was centered on people. This meant seeking out the victims of injustice, bringing exiles back home to Athens, and guaranteeing people's security in their homeland. It meant breaking with the old habit of regarding one's fellow Athenians as mere assets. And, as Solon says, it was accomplished by a leader capable of fitting together the power to get things done with the spirit of justice.

In this first revolutionary phase of Athenian history, an unprecedented, self-conscious community began to emerge, rallying together under its own initiative and inspiring leadership, first against a would-be dictator and then against the selfishness of a powerful few. We see the invention of a basic legal system meant to codify the very new idea that there should be fixed and equal rules for governing everyone's social behavior, and protecting everyone from arbitrary treatment, regardless of personal status. We see the breakthrough concept that no member of Athenian society should be allowed to enslave another member (although not the abolition of enslavement of foreigners). And finally we see the equally extraordinary concept that every member of society should have a vote in deciding what the community, as a community, should do to both preserve and grow itself.

This first set of accomplishments was a huge step toward the invention of citizenship—an identity based on membership in the organization, with certain guaranteed rights and responsibilities. The core value of individuality—security, equality, and freedom for every individual—began to take form as a fundamental principle of the community. The first revolutionary phase began to align values with structure through new practices centered on law and justice. And thus, it put the Athenians on the road to the outstanding performance capacity that would lead to the extraordinary achievements of the classical era, symbolized by the Parthenon. But citizenship was not invented in a day. A second revolutionary phase soon followed—though initially the challenges and solutions seemed to put at risk all that Solon had accomplished.

In the decades after Solon, Athens again suffered civil strife, driven by continued economic change, by incursions from rival city-states, and by a backlash against the new civic freedoms on the part of the old-line aristocratic families. The antidote that first emerged was centralized authority. Consolidated rule by a dynasty of enlightened despots pulled Athenian society back from the brink of civil war once again, albeit with an iron hand. But Solon's reforms were not forgotten. The despots found they could not ignore the early steps toward community-building and the spirit of justice guaranteed by law. Indeed, the nascent civic consciousness and the institutions of civic governance first established by Solon continued to develop under the autocracy. Toward the end of the sixth century B.C., the tyrannical family of despots fell from power in the midst of a series of Spartan invasions of Athenian territory. The Athenian people rallied to save their city once more and took the next giant step toward the invention of citizenship.

REVOLUTION AND REFORM

Some traditional Athenian aristocrats saw the Spartan invasions and the collapse of the tyranny as an opportunity to turn back the clock—a chance to take Athens back to its pre-Solon days, when the big landowners ran everything and ordinary Athenians could be bought and sold as mere assets. However, the aristocrats could not agree on who should serve as leader. As they quarreled with one another, a violent struggle for control of Athens quickly broke out, a struggle that was complicated by the looming specter of external conquest by the Spartans.

The two major adversaries in the conflict, Cleisthenes and Isagoras, were both members of powerful and aristocratic Athenian families. As their contest for control of the community became more bitter, each man was driven to look for new sources of support. Isagoras initially seemed to hold the better hand: In 508 B.C., backed by the rulers of Sparta (who saw him as a tool for Spartan ambitions), Isagoras secured for himself the major executive office once held by Solon. Cleisthenes held no office but he proved to be a far bolder thinker. Like Solon before him, he saw that the challenge faced by Athens required a completely new way of understanding the relationship of individuals to their community. Building on the values embedded in Solon's code of law, Cleisthenes turned to the Athenian populace, promising radical governance reforms that would offer enhanced freedom, equality, and security to each citizen and thereby transform the *politeia.* The Athenian people were ready for such an offer and responded enthusiastically to this enhanced vision of individual potential and community governance. With the people overwhelmingly behind him, Cleisthenes suddenly became the most powerful man in Athens.

In desperation, Isagoras played his trump card by calling in the Spartans for help. Even in these early times, three generations before the great Peloponnesian War of the late fifth century B.C., the Spartans were rightly regarded as the dominant military power in the Greek world. They eyed the Athenians as troublesome neighbors and an obstacle to their control of the Greek mainland. Isagoras' offer to make Athens a part of their subservient league of allies was tempting. Expecting to take control of the Athenian city-state and install Isagoras as a puppet ruler, Sparta dispatched a band of soldiers to the city of Athens. In fear for their lives, Cleisthenes and many of his most influential supporters fled into exile. Within short order, the Spartans occupied the city, and for a while, it looked as if Isagoras had won. But Isagoras and his Spartan allies were soon to meet with a rude surprise—a dramatic change in fortune that would demonstrate clearly the power of the second revolutionary phase in the invention of citizenship.

After driving Cleisthenes into exile, Isagoras and the Spartans methodically began to dismantle the Athenian government, ordering the governing council to disband. But amazingly, the council refused to obey orders. Then, as the Spartans prepared to use force to carry out their plans, they were confronted by a broad-based coalition of Athenians who rose up in arms to defend their organization against the invaders, and to defend the fledgling *politeia* inaugurated by Cleisthenes against a return to narrow oligarchy. Overwhelmed by the speed and size of the insurgency, the Spartan force evacuated the city. Isagoras was driven into exile, Cleisthenes was recalled, and the Athenians suddenly confronted a very different future. They had put their values into action, refusing to accept a return to the situation in which individual Athenians could be treated as other men's assets. And this event opened a whole new world: Citizenship had been invented—even if no one yet knew quite what it fully meant.

The importance of the revolution of 508 B.C. can hardly be overstated. Despite their preeminence as a military power, the Spartans were expelled by the swift and decisive reaction of the Athenians, who were now acting cohesively as a company of citizens. That citizen community was bound together by a fundamental core value of community, willing to take great risks collectively and unwilling to surrender its newfound autonomy to the Spartan nemesis—no matter how fierce its military reputation. As their successful uprising proved, the people of Athens had clearly *become the organization* and proved that they were ready to die to defend it if need be. Upon his return to Athens, Cleisthenes was able to put his revolutionary ideas to work. He had the chance to create the institutions of governance and practices of citizenship that would allow the revolutionary moment to become a way of life, to allow its meaning to expand and take root. The citizens had shown themselves to be their own masters, and now they were ready to implement a new and much more democratic way of working.

But first they would have to face a daunting performance challenge. The Spartans did not take their expulsion from Athens lightly. Angered and humiliated by their unseemly ejection, they soon returned to Athenian territory, this time with a huge army augmented by regiments enlisted from their partner cities in southern and central Greece. They planned a devastating invasion on three fronts. Even a city that had done nothing for the past generation other than prepare for such an attack would shudder at such a threat. And on the surface, with all the recent civic strife and in the midst of fundamental and disruptive changes in its system of governance, Athens looked like an easy target. Instead of succumbing, however, the Athenians delivered an astonishing and crushing military defeat to the invading Spartans and their allies. In the space of just one year, and aided only by their new conception of citizenship and Cleisthenes' visionary leadership, the Athenians had put together a well-organized and passionate fighting force that ultimately thwarted the invaders.

The Athenians overcame this fearsome invasion force by consolidating, virtually overnight, a working company of citizens. Their victory over the Spartans, and the unity of purpose that this victory symbolized, gave them some breathing room at last. Over the next two decades, with their new *politeia* in place, they initiated the power and creativity of a community that would soon defeat the forces of the Persians at the Battle of Salamis, start on the road to an expansive and wealthy empire, and build the magnificent Parthenon. With the invention of citizenship, Athens was on the way to becoming the leading city-organization of the Greek world.[3]

THROUGH A COMBINATION of powerful values and bold action, Cleisthenes and the Athenians created a new structure of organizational governance and revolutionized the concept of the community. They made of themselves genuine citizens, and made citizenship truly meaningful, day to day and over time, through the inauguration of new participatory practices. In so doing, they built an organization that put people in the center of the Athenian universe, and dramatically increased their ability to innovate and perform. The first and most important reforms were put into place in great haste, in the face of the awesome performance challenge represented by Spartan military invasion. Thereafter, the new system developed further through the practical experience of acting in "real time," learning from the outcomes at every step of the way and correcting as necessary. The system's development and refinement continued for almost another two centuries, and as we will see, that long period of consolidation was vitally important. But nothing that came after had the impact of what Cleisthenes and his colleagues accomplished—which was extraordinary and truly revolutionary.

The genius of the solution was not only new ideas about citizenship or new institutions of citizenship, but rather their combination. In fact, the real innovation lay in the dynamic mix of values, structures, and practices. The solution addressed fundamental human potentialities by redefining what it meant to be a free individual and also a member of a community of individuals. The extraordinary speed with which the citizen solution was consolidated might seem to imply that there is some magical secret to building a company of citizens. But there is nothing magical about it: It is a matter of surfacing and rearticulating core values and putting those values into action. This means devising new governance structures. It also means setting in motion the practices that allow the citizens themselves, through their day-to-day experience of the organization, to take control of their own destiny, and through their active participation and accountability, to live the values of free and communal people. We will look at values, structures, and practices in more detail in chapters 4 and 5. But first, we need to explore further Cleisthenes' "revolutionary year"—the historical moment in which democratic citizenship came fully into being.

Let's begin by reflecting on the *imperatives of organization* that, in the context of the historical situation, drove the creation of *citizenship*. We can identify five such imperatives, which also point toward some of the steps that today's leaders will need to embark upon in building modern companies of citizens.

The first organizational imperative faced by Cleisthenes and his fellow Athenians was to *align change around a steep performance challenge*. It is fair to say that the challenge that the Athenians faced was at least as great, if not greater, than that faced by any modern company: If the Athenians failed to meet the challenge of reasserted oligarchic rule and domination by the Spartans, all Athenians would lose their collective autonomy and security as a political community. Most would lose their personal freedom. Many would lose their lives. Cleisthenes first "turned to the people" as a new tactic in the political struggle with aristocratic rivals. But the challenge and need became substantially greater when the specter of foreign domination loomed. The Spartan threat to Athenian autonomy and freedom, and indeed to Athens' very survival as an independent city, exerted enormous pressure on the reformers to devise a new organizational model. That model had to be both effective and comprehensive: It was not only for the armed forces but for the entire community that would be supporting the struggle. The external threat similarly forced members of the community to put aside their internal squabbles and work together. Once underway, the reforms gained momentum as more and more Athenians recognized how high were the stakes of failure—but also of future success. The performance challenge rallied the spirit of *politeia,* a spirit that had been sparked with the reforms of Solon.

The second organizational imperative was to *harness the power of collective action*. The performance challenge demanded that the maximum effort and talent be brought to bear to save Athens. In "turning to the people," Cleisthenes gambled that by making the city more democratic, by establishing a people-based citizenship, the community would become stronger and more able to leverage the knowledge, skills, and resources of a broader and deeper population. Cleisthenes saw that the values of individuality and community could be consolidated with the third great value, moral reciprocity: He brought the people over to his side by convincing them that the community could be redefined as an organization dedicated to the improvement of each individual Athenian. Meanwhile, new structures of governance were quickly put into place. As the framework emerged, the practices of citizenship in turn made the values real to the Athenian population.

In this revolutionary era, the definition of citizenship changed dramatically. Athenians who became citizens were not just those people whose ancestors had long resided in the Athenian territory of Attica. The franchise was now expanded to include many recent immigrants from foreign lands—new homesteaders, mercenaries who had come to Athens to serve in the bodyguard of the tyrants, and traders who had moved there to take advantage of new commercial opportunities. In devising a broad and inclusive model of citizenship, the reformers embraced the conception of an "open architecture of membership."

The third organizational imperative was to *expand and enhance the meaning of "belonging" to a community*—making membership available, real, practical, and emotionally satisfying. Cleisthenes and his colleagues transformed the existing status of "being an Athenian." They gave it deeper meaning, with language and passionate rhetoric celebrating the values of freedom and equality. They also made citizenship more reliable by formalizing the procedure of membership enrollment and certification. In so doing, they were reversing previous aristocratic governance practices based on keeping people in a state of insecurity about their membership in the community. The reformers ended the traditional system under which elite rulers could arbitrarily decide who was *really* an Athenian and kill or exile as political enemies anyone they decided was "un-Athenian." Now it was not some elite ruler but your fellow citizens as a community who guaranteed for you your status of citizenship. You became a citizen through a vote by the citizens, and no one but your fellow-citizens could ever take citizenship away from you. The formalization of that status created a new and stronger sense of individual security. That in turn allowed for the growth of the deep mutual trust on which a true company of citizens must be built.

In addition to formalizing the process of becoming a citizen, reforms during this time also firmly established rights and responsibilities for citizens. Under Cleisthenes' leadership, Athenians were guaranteed the right to vote for war and peace, participate in the process of "ostracism," choose military officers, and pass capital sentences and inflict fines on fellow citizens who committed serious crimes. Citizens over age thirty were also entitled to serve in an important new body: an agenda-setting "Council of 500." Other responsibilities included service in restructured armed forces. Rights and privileges were offset by the expectation that each man would also make important contributions to the community—addressing the human need to justify oneself by "giving" and not just "getting."

The fourth imperative was to *balance the goals of individual autonomy and community responsibility*. Counterpoised to the prerogative of collective action and the sense of loyalty to the organization in a time of danger was the celebration of freedom and equality for every citizen, and thus the opportunity to steer one's own fate as a member of the community. Equality and freedom manifested themselves in the new, more clearly codified set of rights and responsibilities, prerogatives to speak out in the Assembly, and the tolerance for local and individual differences in the society. Autonomy and identity were also manifest in reforms that made villages and neighborhoods a key element of the new organization. The ideals of "equal right to speak out" and "equality before the law," which had been rallying cries of the revolution, now came into being as established cultural norms.[4]

The fifth and final imperative was to *build and define networks of people-to-people relationships,* augmenting old and well-established human networks with new networks based on the practices of citizenship. The Athenians' sense of membership in the society had traditionally been defined by birth into a kinship group, by belonging to one of several so-called "tribes" that were scattered across the countryside. But since the time of Solon, the meaning of traditional tribal membership had blurred, both as a result of increased immigration into Athens and a steady migration of people from the countryside into the central city. Cleisthenes' new organization of citizenship recognized the demographic changes and replaced the traditional and hierarchical structures of tribal kinship with a new concept of membership that reasserted the importance of locality—a different but still familiar and time-tested focus of identity. Yet the familiar idea of working with networks of people in your local neighborhood took on exciting new meaning in the context of a company of citizens.

NEW HUMAN NETWORKS

In the new *politeia,* every male Athenian aged eighteen or over was potentially a citizen of the city on the basis of his membership in a local village or urban neighborhood (called a *deme*). But he was granted membership in his deme only after gaining the approval of his neighbors, expressed in a formal vote. This meant that the local village or neighborhood now became essential for certifying each citizen with his membership identity. Moreover, each of these demes (there were about 140 of them, each with about 100 to 300 citizens) became an elementary unit of local governance. Basing a "national" citizenship on the enrollment in a locality and the judgments made locally was a simple but brilliant innovation. It leveraged the established practical experience of the Athenians in village-level decision making for the much more ambitious purposes of the remodeled city-state organization. The villagers' preexisting, informal practices in neighborhood matters were made more formal with the establishment of responsible officials and regular decision-making assemblies, which assumed authority for regional policies and conflict resolution. The establishment of a deme-based governance structure for the company of citizens was conservative and reformist at the same time: based on existing habits and human relationships in villages and neighborhoods, but by its design also helping to break the habits and relationships based in a legacy tribal system.

The structural changes forced upon the population a host of new relationships, even as it endorsed some old ones. As the existing villages were confirmed as the elementary unit of governance, they were also made part of a larger, new organizational structure that fostered different groups of people working together across all of Athenian territory. As another part of the Cleisthenic revolution, the entire population of Athens was newly distributed into ten new and artificial "tribes." The term was the same as for the legacy kinship groupings, but the new tribes were very different in function. Via selection by lottery, villages from three completely different parts of the Athenian countryside—from the agricultural inland, the seaside, and the urban center—were administratively linked together and assigned to one or another of the ten new tribes. As a result, inland farmers, coastal seafarers, and urban merchants were mixed together into each new tribe. Under the new system, these new tribes became an important basis of both military and civic service with the reformers' intent to mix together citizens from geographically disparate parts of the organization. Bringing together people with different life experiences and skill-sets fostered cross-boundary, working relationships.[5] The genius of the plan is that it built a system of radically new groupings of people (the new tribes) on a foundation of established and time-tested local and personal relationships (the villages and neighborhoods).

This combination of endorsing and enhancing local village governance while combining it with a more broad-based "mixed membership" for activities important to the city as a whole created a citizenship that was both local and national. It also points to the essential role of practices of citizenship in the new solution: The goal was to foster learning at multiple levels in the community, by leveraging the very human vehicles of debate, teamwork, and a rotational approach to leadership. These practices would, at first, function among people who knew one another well (as fellow deme-members), but later these same practices would function among people who did not know one another at all, when they met in "national" institutions such as military regiments or large-scale assemblies. Citizens quickly learned to cross-appropriate practices from the local to the national sphere.

The overall approach of combining familiar and new, local and national, is best described as "building networks of networks"—and it is one of the most important practices typical of a company of citizens.[6] Cleisthenes' breakthrough idea was to increase the scale of knowledge and experience based on linking together microcommunities (the demes) that were repositories of local and specialized skills and experience—such as shipping, farming, building, and fighting techniques—in addition to experience or "social knowledge" regarding the capabilities of other individuals. All this vital local knowledge was then brought together at a national level in the citizen Assembly and other democratic institutions. At its core, the strategy enabled a community to learn faster by taking advantage of the collective wisdom and talents of a diverse but integrated population. Networking was invented as a response of an organization facing an awesome performance challenge: a huge threat to its very survival. The Athenians abandoned traditional top-down governance, and in empowering and putting together thousands of citizens, created a powerful force for both national security and future growth.

In the new organization Athenians learned to be participating citizens through their engagement in the practices of citizenship. We can better appreciate the genius of the "networks of networks" principle and its power in leveraging people-to-people relationships by looking in more detail at one of the fundamental reforms of Cleisthenes, the institution of a new governing council. We focus on the way in which it brought a whole range of citizenship imperatives together in practice. This new "Council of 500" (it enlisted 500 citizens each year) quickly became a hothouse for growing new working relationships, and a key source for learning and teaching the new *politeia*. A close look inside the Council reveals just how practices of citizenship worked to align core values with innovative governance structures.[7]

The new Council comprised deme members from all across the territory of Athens. Each deme was responsible for annually appointing one or more of its citizen-members to a tribal team of fifty men. Every year ten such teams, one from each of the ten new tribes, served for a year on the Council. Because the several demes that made up each new tribe were geographically diverse (inland, coastal, and urban), each team of fifty ultimately reflected the diverse territory of Athens. The full Council of 500 thus brought together teams of citizens from all across the Athenian community and fostered a practice of people working across class, experiential, and geographical boundaries.

The main duties of the Council of 500 were to set and drive the agenda for the national citizen Assembly, which now began to meet more frequently and regularly in central Athens. The Council also discharged other administrative and judicial duties. Cleisthenes saw that the organization needed a standing body that would serve as an official presence—for example, to receive and manage deputations of foreign ambassadors. What was required for these and other civic duties was a living embodiment of the company of citizens, a need the Council now fulfilled. But it was not regarded as necessary to have all five hundred members of the Council on hand at all times: That would be a costly waste of people's time. Instead, just one of the tribal teams was constantly on duty as a presiding team, known as a "presidency," between meetings of the overall Council. This was arranged on a rotational basis, with each of the ten teams taking its turn on active duty as a presidency for a tenth of each year.

The Council members were not legislators (legislation was left to the Assembly), nor were its members representatives— they were not expected to answer to their demesmen or slavishly serve the particular interests of their local constituencies. Rather, the five hundred Councilors chosen each year by their fellow demesmen were the human embodiment of the knowledge-base of the entire Athenian organization. Their duty as Councilors was to bring local knowledge to the "center"—to participate in open discussions, with one another, and with the thousands of citizens who attended any given Assembly. The Councilors were expected to voice and share all the relevant wisdom and experience they possessed, aggregating knowledge and judging how to best serve the needs of Athens as an independent city-state.

The Councilor's experience of working together with Athenians from other demes provided a deep education in the organization as a whole. During his period of service on a presidency, each Councilor would eat and sleep in the same building with the colleagues of his tribe. Throughout his year's service, he would become intimately acquainted with the distinctive experiences and views of other people from diverse parts of his community. A farmer came to understand the importance of overseas trade. A commercial worker gained insight into the ways in which warfare could disrupt the agricultural calendar. A citizen of the coast could share his knowledge of seafaring in decisions about the navy. Each Councilor would take on serious responsibilities, engaging in active debate and making tough decisions. And when he returned home to his village, he would reflect back to his relatives and neighbors both an understanding and a consciousness about how Athenian governance worked at a macro level. Councilorships rotated every year, so year in and year out, more and more Athenians had a chance to learn about their *politeia* through hands-on experience, and through the practice of governing for the common good.

Through this institution and its practices, each individual Councilor learned the value of working intensively and cooperatively on a team, balancing the values of individuality and community. He learned to place his trust in men from very different parts of the organization—a trust based on developing a personal knowledge of them as individuals, and on a shared dedication to the flourishing of the organization to which they all belonged. He learned through his own practice what the value of moral reciprocity really meant. He was experiencing in his own life just how the community benefited the individual. Furthermore, the ten tribe-based teams that made up the Council had to learn in turn to work together. As they dealt with the daily business of Athens, and with the recurrent task of designing an agenda for the meetings of the Assembly, the five hundred Councilors became familiar with how to move from the relatively intimate society of their fifty-member teams to the much larger bodies of the full Council and then to the huge citizen Assembly.

Service on the Council was a practical education in organizational scalability, as well as the meaning of democratic values. Each Councilor participated in making difficult trade-offs that affected both his personal welfare and that of the organization as a whole. He was among the first to receive the reports of generals, ambassadors, and foreign embassies. He helped to conduct elections and votes in the massive citizen Assembly. He carefully scrutinized the accounts submitted by executive officers. He sat in judgment on impeachment proceedings and other legal actions. His time in service on the Council taught him, in detail and through his own day-to-day practice, how self-governance really worked. And along the way he built lifetime networks of trusted colleagues from all across the territory of Athens.

The term for participating in the Council was one year, and the law limited each citizen to no more than two terms of service as a Councilor during his lifetime. Doing the math, we can estimate that pretty much every Athenian citizen who reached age thirty (the minimum age for Council service) had the chance (and frankly the need) to take at least one turn on the Council during his lifetime.[8] Thus, over time, as more and more cross-Athenian networks of people who had worked together in the Council developed, the networks served to integrate and bind together the society. When a Councilor returned home after his year of service, his new understanding of self-governance and his expanded networks of relationships with other Athenians became part of the ever-expanding knowledge base available to his demesmen. And thus knowledge and experience flows were reciprocal, reiterated, and based on earned trust: Knowledge and experience flowed freely and steadily from diverse localities to the governing center, and back from the center to the localities.

Because the new networks based on the practices of citizenship drew from existing networks that flourished at the local level in the demes, the expertise of the citizens as a body developed much more quickly than we might otherwise expect. One of the standard criticisms of participatory democracy is that it is "governance by amateurs." That is partly true, but the engagement and passion that came with "learning by doing" as opposed to more matter-of-fact "professional" leadership was seen by the Athenians as a worthwhile compromise. The risk of the compromise was hedged on two accounts. First, by combining multiple subgroups together, there was an increased chance of the right knowledge coming forward from someone who really knew what he was talking about. Second, because Councilors were drawn from people with local governing experience in the demes, the Council operated not with rank amateurs, but rather citizens who came to Athens with relevant "minor league" experience in local governance.

The "network of networks" design reflected in the organization of the Council of 500 is a theme that ran throughout other institutions and practices in the company of citizens. It accomplished what is in many ways the ultimate organizational imperative: to build knowledge, productivity, innovation, and flexibility among multiple, connected subcommunities without creating a self-serving bureaucracy or a demotivating system of command and control. Cleisthenes' response to the performance challenges his polis faced was to create—by team-building, rotation, and cross-fertilization—an organization that was both "big" and "small," time-tested and revolutionary. And thus Cleisthenes completed the revolution begun in the time of Solon and initiated a true company of citizens. Its legacy was two hundred years of innovation and unusually robust and re-silient organizational performance.

FROM REVOLUTION TO
SUSTAINED PERFORMANCE

The basic structure of the company of citizens was put into place extremely quickly, and the power of the solution was immedi-ately demonstrated as the Athenians pushed back the Spartan invaders who attacked on the heels of Cleisthenes' reforms. Nonetheless, the entire edifice of democratic citizen culture was not completed overnight. In the breathing space opened by their victories over the Spartan rival, the Athenians won precious time to further develop their community, and they used it well in the generation after the revolution of 508 B.C. One tangible out-come (discussed in chapter 2) was the landmark Athenian deci-sion to adopt Themistocles' vision of their new potential as a naval power and resist the Persian invasion at Salamis in 480 B.C. At the meeting that led to that decision, some cautious Athenian elders counseled flight from Athens. But the generation that had grown up after the Cleisthenic revolution was more sure of itself and its new *politeia*—a confidence justified by the great naval victory it ultimately achieved.

In the aftermath of their victory over the Persians, the Athenians turned their amazing energies to expansion into the Aegean. Talented leaders devised the strategic plan that soon led to the creation of the Athenian Empire: a vast Aegean network incorporating nearly two hundred separate communities into the first and only successful imperial power based on a Greek city-state. The material and human resources that flowed to Athens in those years made possible the construction of the Parthenon, and the innovations of science, literature, military power, and cultural institutions.

During the fifth century B.C., inspired by leaders such as Pericles, the Athenians extended and refined their governance structure, enhancing the democratic laws and institutions established by Cleisthenes' reforms. The meetings of the Assembly and its oversight by the democratic Council became more regular and programmatic. The system of citizen-populated jury courts was expanded and developed. And a body of laws was instituted governing the process of judicial decision making. A series of executive offices was established. The elected board of generals came into focus as a center for leadership in military campaigns and foreign policy. Increasingly larger numbers of citizens now regularly traveled to the central city, where they participated in decision making in legislative, judicial, and executive matters, both great and small. By engaging actively in the new institutions, Athenians developed and matured the all-important participatory practices that made citizenship progressively real and vital for every individual.

Also during this time, Athenian thinkers and other Greek commentators who came to Athens were inspired by the practices of participatory citizenship to devise the first critical *theories* of democracy. The principles that underlay the creation and expansion of a company of citizens were explored in the historical writings of Herodotus and Thucydides, and in the teachings of a new generation of human-centered philosophers. The most famous of these was Socrates, who spent his time in the civic square discussing truth, virtue, and their place in a democratic society with anyone willing to subject himself to the philosopher's ferocious intellect and ironic sense of humor. Democratic ideas and principles were also examined, and in some cases even personified, in new dramas presented by the great Athenian tragedians and the comedy of Aristophanes.

Much of this intellectual examination was probing and creatively critical: The Athenians were continuously challenged by the intellectuals of the time to do better, to be more careful custodians of the wealth and extraordinary performance capacities that their approach to organization had brought them. Criticism was not only allowed, but indeed almost always expected. As we will see, there was one devastating exception to this general rule: the trial of Socrates in 399 B.C. We will examine the circumstances of that trial in detail later (see chapter 5). While it is important to recognize that the democratic community was not always true to the principle of encouraging criticism, we must also realize how public and open criticism usually was. The company of citizens paid dramatists with public funds to expose the foibles of institutions and leaders in plays that were presented to audiences that included thousands of citizens.

The practices of democratic culture and participatory citizenship meant that learning, criticism, and innovation went hand in hand. It is not surprising, then, that Pericles, the leader who spoke about "Athens as the education of Greece," is also credited with further democratizing Athenian legal proceedings through

the institution of important reforms such as regular pay for public service. Nor is it surprising that he was often roasted in the
no-holds-barred arena of Athenian comedy. No matter how
much the Athenians accomplished, no matter how insightful
their leaders, the dynamic culture that emerged in the generations after the revolutionary age of Cleisthenes continually challenged the citizens and their leaders to do better.

Criticism of public decisions found ready targets, as the Athenians periodically deluded themselves into believing that, because they could do so much, they could do almost anything. As
we have seen, the desperate struggle with the Spartans in the
great Peloponnesian War (431–404 B.C.) challenged the Athenians to do more with less. And this resulted in some outstanding
displays of the potential of citizen-based performance, typified
by Phormio's naval campaign around Naupactus. But the company of citizens also made serious miscalculations and in the end
it was Sparta that won the Peloponnesian War. The defeat led to
a brief period of civil strife in Athens during which pro-Spartan
oligarchs took control of the city. Yet the values of citizenship
held firm. A counter-coup put the supporters of democracy
back in charge of the city. The crisis of defeat and civil war was
quickly turned into an opportunity for serious reflection on the
nature of democratic governance. A thoughtful series of new institutional reforms was put in place, intended to prevent the sort
of overreaching that had led to the fatal strategic errors of the
latter part of the Peloponnesian War.

And so, despite Athens' defeat by Sparta in 404 B.C., the company of citizens continued to flourish and to enhance its system
of self-governance for almost another century. The Assembly,
councils, and courts continued to meet, and policies and procedures related to governance and citizenship were further refined.

Ongoing wars and foreign conflicts persisted as a backdrop to that constant work of refinement and learning. The lost empire was soon replaced by a more dynamic and market-based approach to commerce, and financial reforms allowed for the growing Athenian expertise in handling public monies to be leveraged more efficiently. The result was Athens' return to prosperity and influence in the larger Greek world. Meanwhile critical reflection and the practice of democratic citizenship continued their mutually reinforcing development of an innovative and resilient community.

Because of the long period of consolidation and evolution, democratic culture developed a depth and richness that allowed it to transcend its original Athenian context. And this meant that democratic culture remained influential long after Athens eventually lost its independence to Macedon and Rome. Citizenship was invented in the time of Solon and Cleisthenes, in the crucible of extraordinary performance challenges. But the company of citizens is available as a model for today's leaders because the organization proved durable, capable of maintaining itself over a long period of time. The Athenian experience in inventing citizenship and sustaining it over time yields several key insights that leaders can put to use today.

As we've seen, events in the early history of Athens, culminating in the crisis of freedom and survival in the time of Cleisthenes, set up the critical need for the community to respond and preserve its sense of self and way of life. A major performance challenge raises the opportunity—and stakes—for a self-governing organizational solution. Cleisthenes put in place a design that drew on history and grew through experimentation. By shaping the values, institutions, and practices that defined democratic citizenship, he created an "answer" to a problem that was literally a life-and-death issue for his fellow Athenians.

Cleisthenes' answer was not the only possible solution, but it turned out to be an unusually powerful one—an operating model of organization that produced high performance and paved the way for continuing innovation. If it had failed, Athens would have fallen under the shadow of Sparta, and many of its citizens would have been put to death. The stakes were high but so also, therefore, was the power of the solution that ultimately triumphed. We close this chapter by reflecting on some lessons for building a modern company of citizens, in light of what the Athenians learned from Cleisthenes and his remarkable legacy.

1. *Design a self-governing organization that leverages the power of people working together.* To leverage the skills, knowledge, passions, and talents of people for maximum impact, one must empower people both as individuals and as members of a community at the same time. Creating such an organization necessitates understanding human needs and aspirations and aligning and motivating people so as to get the very best from them. It requires taking advantage of—and helping every member of the community to understand—the power of collective action. It requires making membership in that community meaningful, by giving each individual a say and sense of authority in steering the activity and results of that community. It demands balancing devotion to community with respect for and development of every individual so each can be the best he or she can be. And it requires building an ongoing and dynamic matrix of human collaborations by networking networks of people.

2. *Lead with vision and values, and make the commitment also to learn from and follow others when it is their turn to lead.* As the careers of Solon and Cleisthenes show so clearly,

leadership in a self-governing organization does not flow from seniority or position in a hierarchy, but rather from vision and a capacity to articulate core values: It is about inspiring others, shaping and reinforcing common beliefs and objectives, and bringing out the knowledge and passion of people. Leaders in a citizen company are also teachers committed to helping others grow into potential leaders.

The Athenian *politeia* was based on the concept that every citizen had to be willing to both rule and be ruled. When the political leader Demosthenes successfully advocated going to war with Macedon, he personally led the diplomatic initiative to build a multicity force. But when the Athenian army headed off to battle, citizen Demosthenes marched in the ranks as an ordinary infantryman—following the orders of the elected generals who were charged with carrying out Demosthenes' policy. The same principle of ruling in turns will help to build a modern company of citizens. It means rotating responsibilities, and accepting the authority of others in turn, even if one does not always agree with everything they do. Ruling and being ruled in turns does not mean totally abandoning hierarchy—Athenian executive officers and military generals, for example, had full command-and-control authority when in office. But their authority was subject to term limits, and could be challenged by legal process if it got out of line with the community's established norms and values.

In the same spirit, the leader in a company of citizens must be willing to take control, accept the consequences of both success and failure in what he or she advocates and drives, and, in turn, give up power to others. There are all too many modern examples of failures in which a leader makes a half-hearted attempt to initiate something like a citizen-style organization, but then refuses to abandon his hierarchical authority when things go differently than he had hoped. There's nothing more counter-productive than a sham revolution. Great Athenian leaders such as Solon, Cleisthenes, Themistocles, and Pericles all suffered setbacks, but they each had the courage of their convictions and each acted on the belief that any attempt to return to a rigid hierarchy would be an admission of defeat for the organization as a whole.

3. *Bring the values of self-governance to life through the creation of institutions and shared practices.* Values such as "freedom," "equality," and "security," or a commitment to make everyone better, are meaningless unless there are mechanisms to translate those concepts and intangible promises into reality. Cleisthenes and his colleagues saw the importance and power of turning those values into deeply felt beliefs and behaviors by giving people the institutions for engaging with the real problems facing the community, and the opportunities to learn and reinforce the feeling of empowerment through ongoing practice. Citizenship was neither an ethereal concept nor a one-time set of legal obligations—it was a continual process of engaged activity and "community sense-making" for every individual.

4. *Start small and local and expand via building networks— both naturally and artificially.* The Athenian revolutionary era demonstrates the power of "grassroots" organizational

development and the value of building on local and human-scale practices as a precursor to bigger and more complex governance. The Athenian inventors of citizenship led a process of self-discovery among the would-be members of the community, and fostered an integration that in many ways followed familiar practices and natural groupings—kinship circles, neighborhoods, and village relationships. But they combined bottom-up and natural practices and groupings with a top-down vision and some deliberately artificially groupings—mixing people from different local centers together and enabling them to work together for common aims and a common good in the national councils and assemblies. As the community's consciousness evolved with the confidence that came with practice, the structured mixing further developed an ever-deeper commitment to the values of citizenship, and empowered the citizens themselves to build out their own community. Small networks became part of larger networks, and the networks themselves drove the continuing evolution.

Builders of today's citizen-centered organization will best follow a similar approach. There's a danger in starting with trying to create an elaborate "constitution" or framework of rights and responsibilities for the "citizens" in some abstract way, devoid of personal meaning and the actual practices of citizenship. As Cleisthenes' experience in devising human networks shows, it is better to work up to a "national" or enterprisewide construct from real decision making and real accountability, on a manageable and human scale. Doing so will maintain the local and personal as part of the ultimate solution—to

keep citizens in touch with relationships and decisions
that are part of everyday life and work. Many modern
organizations have discovered the power of small units
(in the range of 150 or so people). Some even limit the
size of business units and subdivide them if they get too
large.[9] The Athenians first discovered this principle, and
they enforced it not only to preserve the engagement
of people, but also to create forums for the practice of
leadership, learning, and decision making that could be
grown to broader and more significant levels through
higher order networks.

5. *Follow revolution with evolution.* Building anew or transforming an organization into a company of citizens is in
some ways a revolutionary break with tradition and a
common way of working. But it is not something that
can happen overnight, and without advance preparation.
Cleisthenes was able to build a new system of governance
because of the core values that had emerged from Solon's
legal foundation. Themistocles and Pericles in turn refined Cleisthenes' structure, devising new institutions and
practices. Organizations will have to build upon the first
bold steps, with progressive experimentation based on a
growing body of practical experience and knowledge.
For the Athenians, *politeia* emerged through a combination of revolution and evolutionary development. The
process ultimately stretched over a period of almost two
centuries. We believe that the outcome of their process
can be learned and adapted in a much shorter time by
any enterprise looking to learn from their model—but
citizenship is an ongoing enterprise and no one should

fool himself into supposing that the process of building a company of citizens can be completed overnight. It is a journey that must have a commitment for a long horizon, and follow a philosophy of "learning by doing." The iterative interrelationship of values, structure, and practice makes the development of *politeia* by a company an organic and ongoing process. As an individual becomes a citizen, he deepens the meaning and impact of being one through the very practice of citizenship itself.

4

The Passions of Citizenship

A KEY LESSON learned from the Athenians' revolutionary invention of citizenship is the importance of making democratic values real through the creation of structures and practices of self-government. Anyone building a company of citizens today will have to do the same. Today's workers, raised and educated in a broadly democratic culture, tend to take the values of freedom and equality for granted. They expect to be treated as free and equal persons, but they are far removed from the emotional experience of building a system that sustains those values; and for most people in organizations today, those values are not supported by the corporate culture in which they work. To show how self-governance can become a dynamic driver of high-performing cooperative enterprises, we need to further explore the interrelationship between the values, structures, and practices of participatory democracy. We must understand how an ancient Athenian lived and worked in his democratic city, and why and how that experience can be applied to a modern working community. In this chapter we look at the first two pieces of the triad, core values and governance structures, assessing their rationale and interrelationships, and their role in shaping the mindset of the world's first people-centric organization.

AN ICON OF THE PEOPLE

Values and structures represented a vital synergy between the intangibles and tangibles of organizational self-governance. The Athenian community icon—a mature bearded man—symbolized that synergy. The Athenians called him Demos, which translates, quite literally, as "Mr. People." Sophisticated organizations today realize that their brand image (for example the Nike "swoosh" or the classic Coca-Cola script) is not just a marketing ploy, but a powerful symbol that communicates to the firm's clients and stakeholders alike what the company stands for. As with other very successful icons, the image of Demos invited his viewers to participate in a shared identity. He pointed to a way of life, a culture, and an attitude toward the world. In ancient Athens, Demos figured not just as a character in publicly performed political comedies; he was also portrayed in serious official documents. Demos was represented as an individual, a proud citizen with passionate democratic feelings and strong opinions. But he was also, as his name proclaims, a symbolic stand-in for the entire citizen body. As both a citizen and an icon for the entire community of citizens, the image of Demos neatly captures the distinctive Athenian integration of strong-willed individuals and unified community. With his public profile and imagined participatory persona, he forcefully represented the union of the core values, deeply felt by each individual, with the organization's governance structures of execution, justice, and decision making. But just how did these values and structures really come together in the daily life of an Athenian?

The values of citizenship were not passive ideals for the Athenian; they operated as a series of passionate and actionable commitments—commitments to his fellow citizens, to his organization, and to his own sense of identity. These values motivated individual Athenians to spend precious time debating and deliberating with colleagues about the business and strategy of the community. If, for instance, you were a country farmer or coastal fisherman, your commitment to citizenship might compel you to wake up hours before dawn and walk the long miles over the dusty roads from your home village to the civic center. Once there, you further showed your commitment by sitting on a stone bench in an open amphitheater, listening carefully to hours of debate, perhaps raising your voice to contribute your own unique perspective. The commitment also meant casting your vote along with thousands of other citizens—and then accepting the decision that was made, whether you had voted for it or against it. And it meant participating in executing that decision. You did so voluntarily, as a proud member of what you passionately believed to be the world's most talented and innovative organization.

The stakes involved in this sort of fulfillment of personal identity and community destiny were high. The Athenian who willingly spent his time sitting in the Assembly or on a jury knew that the decisions he made could lead to committing his sons— and himself—to bloody armored combat or terrifying naval engagement, risking their lives in brutal battle in a distant part of the Greek world to further Athens' strategic interests. Or it might entail judging that an executive officer had abused the public trust and then choosing how to punish him. It could mean deciding the fate of some fellow Athenian neighbor, someone struggling to keep his family farm in a property dispute. Each of these was a very concrete and real decision that directly affected the individual citizen, the people he cared about most, the city he believed in, and his own sense of self-worth. He wanted to make very sure that the best possible decisions and judgments came out of every meeting of the Assembly and every judicial hearing, because those decisions and judgments affected his own welfare and identity as well that of his community. In earlier times it would have fallen to some aristocrat to make the decisions for him. But the Athenians let stakeholders decide the most important matters for themselves and take on the responsibility for executing the decisions.

Athenian processes of self-governing citizenship were intensely compelling because they effectively engaged not only people's minds, but also their passions. In the course of deliberations people shouted, booed, and laughed. It is not by accident that the same Athenians who invented democratic citizenship also invented the dramatic forms of tragedy and civic comedy. Passion was an engine of commitment and decision making and it ran deeply through the society.

DEMOCRATIC VALUES

The values typical of a company of citizens can seem paradoxical. As we have seen, the practice of democratic citizenship means actively embracing "both/and" thinking. Citizens seamlessly combine cool reason with heart-pounding enthusiasm and a simultaneous focus on personal interests and on the good of the community. Citizens are both fiercely individualistic and highly social, at once materialistic and altruistic. As their visionary leader Pericles pointed out in his Funeral Oration, Athenians were both cultured and courageous. Pericles added that they were proud of their wealth, but their sense of pride did not spring from a love of luxury in and of itself. Rather, wealth was for them a reflection of collective accomplishment and provided the resources for providing benefits to others.[1] Each individual had the opportunity to reap benefits in terms of both material success and emotional satisfaction. Citizens were deeply committed to moral as well as material improvement: to the expansion of public virtue as well as the growth of individual prosperity. The Athenian citizen saw engagement in civic life as a form of personal development, as something positive that increased his potential and qualities as a human being. Each Athenian learned, through the everyday experience of participating in the work of citizenship, what it meant to be an Athenian. They learned, through doing, why "being an Athenian" was an extraordinarily good thing—both for every individual and for the organization overall. And the pride that accompanied that participation was a source of deep passion: As Pericles said, the ideal citizen literally fell in love with his city.

Three Athenian values—*individuality, community*, and *moral reciprocity*—framed democratic self-governance and defined *politeia,* as we mentioned in chapter 1. Because they were deeply embedded in the culture, these values provided the conceptual matrix for the practice of citizenship.

Individuality

Like the modern knowledge worker, the Athenian's understanding of himself began with a serious commitment to the value of individuality, with its three components of freedom, equality, and personal security.

For an Athenian, freedom meant that each citizen was free to participate, to the full extent of his ability and energy, in all the public affairs of the city. The meetings of the decision-making assemblies, at both the local and the national levels, were open and inviting to him. He was free to express his ideas in those assemblies. He was free to dissent and, after debating and listening to others debate, he was free to vote his conscience. He was under no one else's control. Yet freedom also meant that in private life the citizen was at leave to pursue his own interests pretty much as he liked. Pericles alluded to this when he noted that citizens don't give "dirty looks" to their neighbors whose way of life may be in some ways different from their own. Freedom, however, was not just the absence of restraint; it also included a sense of moral expectations. At the heart of the Athenian concept of freedom is a simultaneous embrace of liberty and responsibility—Athenian liberty came with implicit behavioral guidelines.

The citizen was free to act as he wished, but he was not an isolated individual whose actions had no public consequences. Rather he was a member of a community that actively sought to achieve a higher purpose. This "both/and" approach to freedom proved highly productive because it was linked to innovation. The Athenian enjoyed freedom of speech: He was at liberty to speak out in public if he felt that his ideas might further the public good. But beyond that, if he had good ideas, he felt a moral responsibility for making them known. The commitment of each citizen to freedom of speech directly benefited all members of the community, who embraced the manifold opportunities of learning from one another that free expression opened up.

The second component of individuality was equality. Each citizen enjoyed an equal right to participate in public affairs—an equal right to engage in public speech and to stand for public office. His vote in elections or public meetings was equal to that of all others. Equality also meant that all Athenians were regarded as equal in the eyes of the law: Aristocrats could not expect to get special treatment in the courts because of their family connections or deep pockets. Each Athenian had an equal right of appeal to the law if he were subjected to any kind of abuse by one of his fellows. And when there was a trial, the citizens in conflict would be judged by a jury of their equals: a substantial and randomly selected cross-section of the citizen population. Once again, however, there was a trade-off: Equality meant that each citizen shared an equal opportunity to benefit the community, not that each person's opinion would be regarded as equally valuable on every subject. Commitment to equality gave each an opportunity to participate, but always in the service of finding the best solution overall—and accepting the solution even when it wasn't exactly as hoped for.

The third component of individuality was security. Each citizen was protected from coercion and from the sort of deliberate physical or verbal insults that would make it impossible for him to enjoy either freedom or equality. If someone had to live in fear for his life or his status as a member of the citizen community, if he had to put up with the risk of being harmed or insulted in a way that compromised either his well-being or his dignity, he could not be truly free or equal. Thus citizens, as members of a community devoted to the common good, would band together to protect one another from external threats to their city's security, but they would also come together to protect each other against vicious behavior on the part of any aberrant internal member. The public good depended on the collective protection by the community of each of its members. The Athenians were protected by the establishment of processes to challenge public and private wrongs through appeal to the community itself—in the form of a jury of free and equal citizens. Citizens could also count on the support of the community in times of crisis, which enabled the individual citizen to engage in inherently risk-laden activities such as war. The Athenian knew, for example, that if he were killed in battle, his surviving sons would be raised and educated by the community. Secure in this knowledge, he was free to support, with his vote and with his willingness to carry it out, the policy that seemed best overall—even if that policy would put him personally at risk.

Community

For the Athenians, the value of individuality was closely related to the value of community. The community values are most clearly expressed in the conviction that "the people *are* the organization and the organization *is* the people." That deep conviction provided a fundamentally democratic baseline; it acknowledged the centrality of the citizens themselves in the definition of the community that they constituted. This centrality was expressed in the very way the ancient Greeks spoke about their city-states. Today, we tend to speak of the community as "Athens" (as in "Athens went to war . . . ") but in ancient times Athens was strictly the name of the place. The political community was always referred to as the people themselves: "The Athenians" (so "The Athenians went to war . . . "). In both theory and practice, the community could abandon its physical location and remain who it was—as the Athenians did when they left their homeland and took to their warships before the battle of Salamis, as described later in this chapter. In the final analysis, even the ships were just things; it was the people themselves that mattered. As an Athenian general famously said on the eve of another major battle, "Not walls, not ships but men make our community." [2] And in fact the Athenians totally reconstituted their company of citizens after losing most of their material goods—including their warships—after the Peloponnesian War.

Contrast this genuinely people-centered commitment—the active belief that "the citizens are the company"—to the hollow drumbeat of modern corporate annual reports. All too often these insist that "people are our business," while tacitly assuming that the corporate entity stands as something outside and separate from the people, outside the character and commitments of its workers. For ancient Athenians, any separation of the organization from the citizens themselves was unthinkable. That does not mean that Athenians believed their city-state would not thrive beyond the lifetimes of any particular group of citizens—rather they recognized that their city's identity and true nature was inseparable from the people who made up its *politeia*.

Moral Reciprocity

The third essential value of a company of citizens is moral reciprocity: the conviction that the organization serves a vital mission as an educator of each of its individual members, who in return offer the organization their own best efforts. Just as Pericles boasted that Athens was an "education for all Greece," so too the Athenians believed that the Athenian *politeia* was itself an education for all Athenians. Laws were seen not merely as a means of preventing wrongdoing, but also as a means of educating the citizens in virtue, and making every individual a better person.[3] Being a citizen in Athens entailed an ongoing process of mutual instruction: As a member of the community, the citizen was both learning for himself and teaching others the arts of politics, problem-solving, and moral decision making; each citizen was at once a student *and* a teacher to his colleagues. The learning and teaching was "on the job" and action-driven, whether he was fighting together with others in the army or the navy, discussing public issues in the public square, or listening and speaking in the democratic forums of justice and decision making. Each Athenian became familiar with both the values and real workings of the institutions of governance through the specific participatory practices detailed in the next chapter. The core lessons he taught and learned as he participated in the business of his city were consistent: the value of collaboration, learning, and open debate to solve problems and make continuously better and actionable decisions; the importance of shared values in fostering that kind of collaboration; and an ever-deeper understanding of how the goals and aspirations of individual and community were mutually and continuously aligned.

THE VIRTUOUS CYCLE OF SELF-GOVERNANCE

The Athenians' people-centered approach to governance may initially appear to underplay the role of dynamic leadership and offer insufficient rewards for accomplishment. It is still common in contemporary business, as in society at large, to focus quite narrowly on the individual achievements of outstanding leaders; to measure success and power by the single standard of personal wealth; and to see charismatic leadership as the answer to most organizational problems. How did the Athenian company of citizens achieve excellence and results without creating a cult of celebrity around each of their most successful leaders and without making material gain the metric of accomplishment? How did they balance meaningful recognition for outstanding individual achievement with a deep commitment to equal opportunity for all and broad-based participation in self-governance?

The Athenian commitment to civic equality did not require everyone to be a leader. Nor did it imply that citizens should be financially equal to one another. The Athenians expected talented people to take leadership positions, and they expected wealthy citizens to contribute generously of their time and resources to the public good. Those who did so were rewarded with public honors. The assumption, both tacit and explicit, of the company of citizens was that talent and wealth were resources for civic service, not objects for forced redistribution. The balance between civic equality and financial inequality was another dimension of Athenian "both/and" thinking: the citizens both enforced equality of access to civic roles and encouraged entrepreneurial individuals to make private fortunes. The individual's commitment to the community ensured that some part of private success—which the culture of the community had helped foster—was reinvested in the community. Rich people built up social capital through material contributions and public service, and under the right conditions—if the community deemed contribution and service to be at the right level and offered in the right spirit—social capital could translate into influence in the community. But gaining political clout in Athens was genuinely democratic in that it meant winning the public support of thousands of well-informed ordinary citizens—not merely, as is often the case today, winning the personal backing of a few members of a board of directors or contributing to the election campaigns of a few lawmakers.

The Athenian company of citizens functioned in many ways as a free market of ideas. New ideas were offered in the assemblies; the audiences either "bought" the idea or they rejected it in favor of a better one. The man whose idea "sold" the audience was rewarded with public honors; he accumulated social capital. But in other ways Athens was more than an open market. Democratic values protected desirable moral attributes that unregulated internal markets can undermine—including the dignity of weaker individuals and the rights of dissident minorities and outspoken critics.[4] The citizen was expected always to consider whether his behavior would impinge on his neighbor's fundamental sense of honor and identity. He was expected to avoid coercive behavior, even if he was strong enough, smart enough, and rich enough to dominate his less successful fellows. Freedom didn't give anyone in Athens the right to lord it over others. Citizen dignity was further protected in symbolic ways. For example, each citizen was free to amass private wealth, but he was expected not to flaunt that wealth in an ostentatious way in public. Athenians separated the freedom to gain wealth from its most obnoxious social trappings; as Demosthenes once pointed out to his fellow citizens, even great leaders like Pericles lived in relatively modest houses. Wealth did not translate automatically into political influence or social capital, in part because the commitment to personal freedom was tempered by a commitment to civic equality.

Just as their strong commitment to equality resisted the equating of conspicuous consumption with accomplishment without turning the Athenians in the direction of state socialism, nor did it discourage the emergence of effective leadership.[5] A common concern about democracy is that it cannot guarantee that the most capable people, rather than demagogues or smooth-speaking charlatans, gain positions of responsibility. And so, as critics of democracy have often pointed out, decisions may be dragged down to the "lowest common denominator." Yet the Athenians were keenly aware of the need for high-quality leadership—after all, their lives as well as their livelihoods depended on good decisions. That they could build a huge empire and magnificent public monuments, gain military victories, and resiliently respond to setbacks proves that they did indeed find good leadership. But they did not assume that any given leader would hold all the answers or that any one person's ideas would always be best. Athenians accepted the fundamentally experimental character of democracy. In support of both innovation and learning, their model of citizenship held that no one—no matter how much he knew—would always get to set the agenda or determine the outcome for key decisions. Athenians accepted some randomness and variation—and even failure—in the ongoing drive to discover the best answer in each circumstance. But, as we will see, they also instituted strict accountability procedures to make sure that failed experiments did not get repeated. Leadership positions rotated frequently and leaders were subject to regular scrutiny in public forums.

Moreover, as the philosophers Plato and Aristotle pointed out, the company of citizens was extraordinarily sensitive to the importance of expertise. Plato noted that when the citizens were debating in the Assembly about technicalities of shipbuilding, they refused to listen to anyone but competent individuals, such as naval architects. And Aristotle adds that the decision-making process was based on trusting one's neighbor's special knowledge and paying close attention to how the most knowledgeable colleagues on a given topic responded to whatever idea was being put forward on that topic.[6] For example, if a neighbor, a well-respected carpenter, started laughing as soon as an Assembly speaker said that "we can easily find local timber for building new ships, without resorting to foreign imports," one would have known right away that the speaker was sadly misinformed. If that misinformed speaker tried to harangue the Assembly, he would be quickly booed off the podium. Freedom and equality together produced not only good-enough decisions, but also ever-better decisions, informed by the most knowledgeable citizens.

New ideas were constantly brought forward in public forums and constantly subjected to the test of knowledgeable public opinion. Yet because the company of citizens also saw itself as an educator, it functioned both as a marketplace of ideas and as a learning community, building its collective knowledge base with each public meeting. The company of citizens was constantly balancing between being open to innovation and experimentation on the one hand, and on the other leveraging tradition—building on shared values and a shared sense of purpose. It is a balance that all organizations have to find if they are to reach their full potential. Getting the balance right can mean great gains in productivity, as the Athenians themselves understood from the first. The Greek historian Herodotus famously wrote: "How noble is *equality of public speech!* . . . [W]hen they were ruled by tyrants, the Athenians did not stand out from their neighbors in military capability, but after deposing the tyrants, they became overwhelmingly superior."[7]

The values typical of a company of citizens stand in stark contrast to the culture of many modern, hierarchical organizations, whose workers are all too often governed by negative passions. Living in fear, they labor to protect their turf and do whatever they have to, no matter how counterproductive or humiliating, to stay on the good side of the boss. That is not to say that hierarchy is necessarily bad. In Athens, some individuals were clearly more powerful than others: they commanded great financial resources, held respected leadership positions, and had well-connected friends. Those holding formal positions of authority expected their orders to be carried out. But the community collectively understood that authority must be exercised under a shared set of beliefs about justice and fairness. If weaker individuals lived in fear of arbitrary treatment or retribution by the stronger, freedom and equality would be empty words; the advantages of innovation that arose from free expression would quickly disappear and productivity would decline. In Athens the hierarchies that emerged from inequalities of talent and wealth were balanced by a fundamental respect for the dignity of each citizen.

In contrast to a company of citizens, the operating assumption of organizations that are based *entirely* on the principle of hierarchy is that security for the weak must be bought through the practices of patronage and clientship throughout the chain of command. The weaker individual accepts the protection of the stronger, but in turn becomes a client and asset—meaning that the client must do his patron's bidding when so commanded. When people act out of fear—when they are forced to accept some version of the Mafia's proverbial "offers you can't refuse"—productivity and innovation suffer. Belief in the organization as a moral community disappears; personal agendas become the reigning principle. Notably, in democratic Athens there was no network of personal patron-client relationships. Because security was guaranteed by direct appeal of individuals *to* the community, individual citizens were eager and willing to do favors *for* the community. The organization looked after the individual as the individual looked after the organization, and both got better and stronger through their mutual education. That positive and reciprocal relationship created a virtuous cycle between the growth of the innovative individual citizen and the productivity of the learning community.[8]

STRUCTURES OF GOVERNANCE

The tangible structures of governance in ancient Athens both manifested and reinforced the rich matrix of democratic citizen values. These structures—processes and institutions of decision making, judgment, and execution—provided the arenas in which the passions of the citizen were translated into effective policy. They were the means through which the citizen learned to link belief with action and reflection with operational follow-through. They were the places where passionate, values-driven, committed people gained access to the means of steering their own collective destiny. In ancient Athens, advances in the intangible concepts and values of democracy were quickly translated into tangible institutions, including assemblies, jury courts, and executive offices. Likewise, advances in the tangibles in turn sharpened and enlivened the values embraced by the citizens. Together they added up to a dynamic and flexible system that could sustain organizational performance day to day and year after year. Here we present a model of governance structure based on the best-documented period of Athenian institutional development: the age of the prominent speaker and political leader Demosthenes.[9]

The structures of self-governance fall into three categories: *decision making* (institutions and processes for deciding among options involving opportunity and risk), *judgment* (institutions and processes for fairly resolving conflict), and *execution* (institutions and processes for carrying out decisions and judgments). All of the structures were fundamentally democratic; the operations and processes depended centrally on the participation of large numbers of citizens and were, at some level, open to all. Yet in each of these core structures there is a prominent role for extraordinary leadership: Policy and strategic options were devised, and the attendant opportunities and risks were carefully weighed, in arguments advanced by trusted leaders like Pericles. Judgments to resolve conflict were based on laws promulgated by wise leaders such as Solon and on the legal arguments developed by leading orators such as Demosthenes. Dynamic generals and statesmen such as Themistocles carried out strategic or operational decisions. Yet in each arena the citizens themselves always played a decisive role. The company of citizens made the final choice, based on the recommendations advanced by leaders who had earned the community's trust.

Decision Making

The involvement of large numbers of people in high-level decision making—in making real choices among options that involve substantial risks as well as substantial opportunities—is a distinctive feature of any company of citizens. Risk-laden decisions include matters in which the organization as a whole assumes a risk, but also include matters that may create a serious disadvantage for some individual citizens in favor of the long-term good of the whole organization. In ancient Athens this meant, for example, voting to go to war, knowing full well that some of the citizens who marched or sailed out to battle would not return home. In modern firms, the most difficult decisions will include such things as accepting salary cuts or layoffs for some workers; or they might be about strategic decisions that "bet the company," putting its very survival on the line. The experience in making tough decisions, and the knowledge that the decisions are made openly and fairly, builds trust and allows the community to rebound from setbacks.

The major decision-making institutions in Athens were the policy-making assemblies (particularly the great national Assembly open to all citizens), along with the councils (particularly the Council of 500), whose purpose was to manage agendas and processes. These councils and assemblies played a key role in maintaining the all-important alignment of individuals and their community. The national Assembly met some forty times a year in a purpose-built and acoustically remarkable amphitheater near the central public square (Agora) of Athens. It was open to all Athenian citizens. A typical meeting drew between six thousand and eight thousand citizens—or roughly a quarter of the citizen body. Attendance was not mandatory, but the Athenians insisted on a quorum whenever critical questions were being decided, for example a proposal to offer citizenship to a foreigner. There was a tacit expectation that the citizen should attend at least some sessions, and when he did so it was expected that he would participate freely.

Each session of the Assembly began with the herald's invitation to the assembled community: "Who has advice to give?" The agenda for business and proceedings were moderated by a team selected from the rotating "presidency team" of the Council of 500. Discussions were open and debate was vigorous, but the goal was to discover the best answer and gain as much consensus as possible for each decision. The Assembly's operation built and reinforced leadership qualities: There was a strong bias to listen to people who had proved their reputation as being the most well-informed, well-prepared, and well-intentioned speakers, capable of persuading and encouraging productive action. Assemblies, both local and national, moved questions to a decision as quickly as possible, while still respecting the importance of discussion to surface important views and information. Every citizen knew that, after a decision, he would be expected to support it and work to implement it. Decisions represented the will of the people, and because the people were the organization, the collective decision was always the "official" one. The participatory process ensured that individual citizens were consistently kept in close alignment with ongoing decisions and thus with Athenian strategy and policy overall. As we'll see in the next chapter, bad decisions could be and were challenged, but unless and until that happened, any decision made by the national Assembly of the company of citizens was expected to hold.

The councils and assemblies were a primary locus of network-building and education; participation in these public forums reinforced existing relationships between people and fostered new ones. Through the processes of citizens speaking, listening, and acting together—through the constant practice of conscientious and action-oriented deliberation—the civic pride and identity of every Athenian was developed in session after session. At the moment of decision making, as he raised his hand in favor of a proposal he had participated in crafting, the value of community—the conviction that "the people are the company"—became tangible to each citizen. He now grasped that idea rationally, emotionally, and physically—with his mind, his heart, and his upraised hand. Participation in assemblies and councils also built commitment and trust between fellow citizens and the decisions they all stood for. If there was a major opportunity, and with it a major risk, facing the community, the citizen knew he would have the chance to take part in its pursuit, and indeed in the consequences of success as well as failure. If there was a particularly hard or dangerous choice—say to commit oneself or one's sons to a battle for defense of a far-distant Athenian ally—the citizen also knew he had no one to praise or blame but himself and his fellow citizens for the outcome. This fundamentally human truth—that maximum alignment is achieved only when actors and decision makers are one and the same—has fueled case after case of constructive "participatory management" in modern companies facing life-or-death decisions.[10] It's a universal of decision making that does not change.

Judgment

Judgment structures included formal laws (written rules) and a range of highly participatory courts and arbitration processes. These institutions and processes also included and depended on a strong tradition of unwritten customs. Taken together, all of these facets represented a system of citizen-centered justice that combined the formal and informal in a powerful way, aligning individual beliefs and behaviors with a commitment to preserving the established traditions of the community.

With the reforms of Solon (discussed in chapter 3), the Athenians first created a body of general laws that maintained order, purpose, and protection for individual citizens and the city overall. These laws were expressed in simple and ordinary language—for example, "you may not commit outrage, in word or deed, against anyone living in Athenian territory." [11] The actual definition of key terms (such as "outrage") and the application of the measures (how to punish the outrageous individual) were left to the judgment of one's fellow juror-citizens as they participated in the justice system. Over time, more laws were enacted, but their impact was always determined by how the citizens, having listened to the stories on both sides of a dispute, chose to interpret a given statute. In the Athenian company of citizens there were no authoritative "judicial experts" to tell the jurors how to interpret the law, nor a formal system of definitive precedents determined by judgments in previous cases. Rather, the citizens trusted one another to make the best judgment under the circumstances; they depended on a common sense of the spirit of formal law and informal custom, an appreciation for the overall context of any trespass or violation, and a requirement for timely application. The goal was to make a judgment within a predetermined period, expect the litigants to accept the consequences, and then let the community move on.

The actual machinery of justice, like the language of the law, was relatively simple. Most disputes among citizens were solved quickly and informally, by presenting the matter to arbitrators who sought to resolve the matter on the basis of their best understanding of the facts (as presented by the disputants) and their inherent sense of equity. Every Athenian who survived to old age could expect at some point in his life to serve as a dispute arbitrator: It was a role that required a basic sense of fairness and long experience in the life of the organization, rather than special legal expertise. The system of citizen-arbitrators depended on the relatively high level of trust among citizens, and a general sense that the individual arbitrator would judge fairly and impartially.[12]

If a matter could not be solved by arbitration, it was sent to trial and was judged by a broad cross section of citizens. Jury panels were large, generally two hundred or five hundred citizens, and always chosen by lot. Decisions about justice were predicated on the values of community, which required a body of citizen-jurors large enough to stand in for the organization as a whole. Every trial featured a concerned citizen who took the initiative in acting as voluntary prosecutor, filing a charge against someone who was thought to have done wrong—to have harmed an individual or the community. The person so charged was expected to defend himself in person before his fellow citizens, sitting in the capacity of jurors.

Unlike lengthy and lawyer-centered modern litigation processes, the Athenian system combined efficiency with high levels of active citizen participation. Once a trial began, time limits were strictly imposed, with even the most serious trials limited to only one day. The society recognized that it was important that justice be handled by citizen peers, but also that the citizens had other things to do. They had to make decisions promptly so that they could all get back to their lives and livelihoods. Professional lawyers were unknown; volunteer prosecutors and defendants represented themselves, and water clocks were used to ensure that each litigant had equal time to present his case. Each side gave its best argument—in exactly the time allotted. Arguments were followed by a secret ballot vote. The votes were publicly counted and simple majority decided the verdict. Frivolous prosecutions, which typically failed to convince a substantial minority of the juryman-voters, carried a stiff penalty for the prosecutor. The Athenians believed that a volunteer prosecutor should be sure enough of his case to take on some personal risk before pressing charges in court.

Trials in Athens lacked the highly formalized language, black robes, and time-consuming formalities and courtesies of Anglo-American court proceedings. Participants were experienced amateurs, not professionals. The democratic courts were a forum in which a man could make his name and build social capital, or lose his fortune and even his life. The community as a whole was deeply involved in judgments, the effect of which was to make the principles and system of justice intensely meaningful and educational for all participants. The Athenian court system was a primary and very practical manifestation of the value of moral reciprocity: the idea that the daily experience of the organization should be an education for each of its members, and that each citizen in turn owed the community his best efforts.

Execution

Execution, the offices and roles for turning decisions into action, will seem familiar territory to every experienced manager.

But the values of the Athenian company of citizens were embodied in particular executive structures that would be unfamiliar to
many managers today. First, in ancient Athens, there was much
less separation between deciding and doing than one finds in organizations today. An Athenian leader who developed and advocated major policy proposals in the Assembly would expect to
play a central role in actually implementing what he had argued
for. For example, when an Athenian political leader named Cleon
publicly advocated a bold new approach to resolving a standoff
with a body of Spartan warriors barricaded on an island, the Assembly immediately assigned him a military command. Cleon himself mustered the necessary troops and brought home the Spartan
prisoners—and did so on the aggressive schedule he had boasted
to his fellow citizens would be both possible and desirable.[13]

Moreover, while many modern companies today embrace
the rhetoric of widely distributed leadership, the Athenian company of citizens vitally depended on it. Democratic Athens employed hundreds of citizens each year in day-to-day leadership
positions, ranging from financial and commercial officials to military generals. Most of them served on teams (typically of ten
people), which served to correct for inexperience and to enhance learning among the members. In all, some 2 to 5 percent
of the citizen population spent time serving on an executive
team in any given year; and with term limits and other rotational
practices, the experience of taking on a leadership role moved
systematically through the citizen population. Dozens of executive teams were charged with specialized duties: public works,
financial accounting, weights and measures standards, minting
money and detecting counterfeits, and so on. In addition, the
community benefited from a wide range of citizen-volunteered
services (for example, hosting a festival or outfitting warships)
Those who managed and performed these services with flair and

public spirit were amply repaid with public honor and the social capital of fellow citizens' esteem.

A challenge for any organization that develops and depends on a broad-based executive group is how to ensure that sufficient knowledge and experience is available when and where it is needed. The Athenians recognized that some executives had to be highly competent and deeply experienced to ensure success for all: Generals, public works engineers, and other expertise-essential functions were selected (usually by vote) from among the subset of people genuinely able to carry out these offices with distinction. But the Athenians also recognized that many executive functions could be filled perfectly well with "experienced amateur" officers. And they saw the value of engaging a wider range of people (usually selected by lot), thereby creating broader-based growth and learning.

By spreading its executive responsibilities widely, Athens never developed a formal bureaucracy. With very few exceptions, all public positions of responsibility, no matter how small or how significant, turned over regularly. Office holders were either elected (for high-stakes responsibilities) or chosen by an open lottery. The democracy of opportunity was balanced by the democracy of accountability. Officials were subject to careful scrutiny, and were liable to prosecution (again, by the body of citizens assembled as jurors) for mismanagement, egregious failure, or moral lapses during their time in office. Because executive positions were grouped into panels or teams, coaching and learning was built into each citizen's executive experience. Team-based leadership also mitigated the risk of an inexperienced individual officeholder making a disastrous mistake. Leadership development at various levels, and through networks of networks, touched thousands of citizens every year.

The broad-based approach to leadership reflected and reinforced the Athenian commitment to equality: Everybody was regarded as capable of some good and given the chance to show that "on the job." The expectation was that each citizen would get better at both leadership and followership by practicing them. As long as the expertise was available in the citizenry, and could be tapped through debate and conferences, Athenians believed there was great social and individual benefit in granting more citizens the opportunity to help steer the organization.

Executive opportunities were a complement to a citizen's regular participation in the assemblies, councils, and courts. The assemblies and juries, in which Athenians made risk-laden decisions on policy and decided matters of justice, were filled with men who had also served, at some level, as executive officers of the organization. They brought deep knowledge of some part of the organization to bear, and became trusted experts whose reactions to proposals made by public speakers were noticed and respected by their neighbors. Once again, we see a virtuous cycle of experience and learning, as executive knowledge was cross-appropriated into the contexts of decision and judgment. By our best estimates, taking all of the leadership, judicial, civic, and military participation opportunities together, an average Athenian may have spent some 25 percent of his adult life in activities related to the self-governance and defense of the city.[14] Because public service was rightly understood as contributing directly to enhancing the potential of each autonomous individual and to his opportunity for living the good life, time spent on public service was never regarded as wasted or misspent.

PASSION AT WORK

We can get a better of idea of how values and structures worked together in real time by looking at the decision-making process that led up to the success story we considered in chapter 2: How did the Athenians actually make the remarkable decision to put their lives and the very survival of their organization on the line in a high-risk naval battle at Salamis?[15] It was a decision that led to triumph over the mighty invasion forces commanded by the King of Persia, the creation of the Athenian empire, and the emergence of Athens as the premier city-organization of Greece. The story behind the decision reveals the true character of the company of citizens through the process of passionate deliberation.

We begin with the context of that all-important decision. The year is 480 B.C.; the eastern King is leading his mighty army and navy in a bid to take over all of Greece. The Persians had just broken through the main line of Greek land defenses at the pass of Thermopylae in northern Greece. With the fall of Thermopylae, the Athenians had only a few brief weeks to devise a strategy against the final invasion. The Persians were heading south, aiming at Athens, by both land and sea. Athenian planning and decision making had to be swift. Bad judgment or delay would mean the end of their freedom—and probably their lives.

Faced with this crisis, the Athenians did not panic nor rush immediately into a full decision-making Assembly. Instead, they opted to gather more information, by sending a delegation to the famous oracle of Delphi. By tradition, the oracle was seen as a source of wise, albeit often ambiguous, advice, dispensed by its divinely inspired priestesses. But equally important, Delphi was also a meeting place where Greeks and foreigners gathered to exchange the latest news and ideas.

When the Athenians asked the oracle what they should do in response to the Persian threat, the answer was ambiguous indeed. At first the message seemed to be that the Athenians were doomed if they chose to fight against the enemy. Then, upon closer questioning, another response came forward: "[T]he wooden wall will not fall, but will help you and your children." But the oracle also prophesied "divine Salamis [the island off the Athenian coast] will bring death to women's sons." The Athenian envoys recorded the oracle's responses and returned to Athens. Now the decision-making Assembly was called. The citizens gathered to hear from the envoys, to listen to leaders, and to make a decision that would surely decide the fate of their community. However they decided, many citizens would suffer and some would surely die.

The Assembly debate quickly narrowed the choices to two: armed resistance or leaving Greece to start a new community elsewhere. The ambiguous oracle provided a heuristic focus for the debates. Some of the most senior Athenians argued that, by "wooden wall," the oracle pointed to the construction of a wooden palisade around the sacred hill of the Acropolis, the natural fortress in the center of Athens—and they advocated building that kind of defense. Others thought that the oracle's message was metaphorical—that the "wooden wall" referred to the great fleet of wooden warships that the Athenians had recently built. Thus the debate was engaged: Flee or resist? And if they were to resist, should they fight on land from the hilltop, or risk a naval battle, looking to their warships to win the day?

The debate then took another turn as specialist opinions came forward: Athenian elders urged against challenging the mighty Persian forces. They were backed up by expert oracle-interpreters who claimed that "divine Salamis bringing death" meant that Athens would certainly be defeated if they dared to risk a naval engagement. But the elders and specialists in oracle interpretation were challenged by other kinds of experts in the assembly: the many citizens who, by their professions and experience, knew a great deal about Athenian naval capability. Other speakers weighed in on the enthusiasm and dedication to the community of the thousands of Athenians who had become citizens through the recent democratic revolution of Cleisthenes.

Next, Themistocles, himself well experienced in naval affairs, stood up to address the Assembly. He directly challenged the elders and the oracle-experts, suggesting that since the oracle had described Salamis as "divine" (rather than "hateful") it must mean that it was the *Persian* invaders who would find their deaths there. And Themistocles complemented his interpretive cleverness with a coherent plan for engaging in naval battle—a plan that took full account of the recent growth of the Athenian fleet of warships and the highly motivated mass of recently enfranchised citizens serving as naval personnel. Themistocles' strategy, grounded in the values of individuality, community, and moral reciprocity, would make optimal use of all available Athenian manpower, rallying the community behind a policy that would not require them to abandon themselves to become passive victims of fate. The decision to man their ships and engage in naval attack called for extraordinary levels of trust, cooperation, and willingness to sacrifice on the part of all Athenians. That was made possible by the new concept of citizenship that had been evolving through the experience of participatory self-governance in the generation since Cleisthenes and the democratic revolution.

Themistocles' plan was based squarely on "both/and" thinking. Themistocles combined the two options earlier discussed— abandon Athens (as a place) *and* resist by naval force. Themistocles proposed that the entire population of Athens leave their homes, with women and children resettling in camps in southern Greece, away from the advancing Persian invaders. At the same time, virtually the entire adult male population was to embark in the new Athenian fleet as rowers and marines, to meet the Persians in the narrows off Salamis. There, in the turbulent straits, superior Persian numbers and the advantage of their greater open-water tactical experience would be minimized. It was a bold plan, fraught with risks. If the Athenian navy lost the battle, all would indeed be lost, since the Persians would then sweep into southern Greece, capturing the rest of the population and moving on to dominate all other Greek cities. It was a plan that required extraordinary execution: It required thousands of citizens to facilitate a rapid and massive evacuation of family members, collaborate to outfit the ships, and steel themselves for the battle. It depended on an extremely high level of trust among a socially diverse body of Athenians.

The plan prevailed and was enthusiastically endorsed by the Assembly. The Athenians, who had supported the proposal with their own votes, put everything on the line—their lives, livelihoods, families, and future. They willingly abandoned their ancestral homeland to the ravages of foreign invaders because they recognized that it was people, not a particular place, that constituted the heart of their organization. The democratic process of decision making completely aligned the deliberators and the executors. A few days later, fired with the passionate sense of their own capabilities, they went on to smash the enemy with an astonishing victory at sea. In the following years, emboldened with success and an ever-growing confidence of what their citizen organization was able to accomplish, the Athenians continued to expand across Greece, rising in power, wealth, and cultural accomplishment unprecedented in the ancient world.

THE ATHENIAN EXPERIENCE demonstrates the power of collective action when pursued through the full alignment of individual and community, and the mutually reinforcing power of democratic values and governance structures. Workers in the modern firm do not usually face the sorts of life-and-death decisions that the Athenians did day to day. But they do confront very tough issues in today's global economy: pushing every day to be faster-better-cheaper than the competition, struggling to innovate, accepting downsizing and leveling pay cuts, sacrificing personal time with family and friends to gain a final edge over a rival firm. Building a modern company of citizens can provide the deeper sense of commitment and ownership that allows people to make tough decisions and to live with their consequences, offsetting the cynicism and resentment that inevitably develop when hard choices are imposed from above.

We suffer today from such thin and deracinated concepts of citizenship, governance, and community that it may be difficult to make the conceptual leap necessary to translate the vivid political passions of the ancient city-state to the bottom-line concerns of a modern business firm. But the same principles that allowed the Athenians to build a highly effective company of citizens are equally valid today: In a modern company of citizens, as for the classical Athenians, every major decision is understood in terms of its personal impact upon the individual. By the same token, every individual is committed to the common good because of his powerful, engaged sense of how much is at stake, both for himself and for the community that contributes so much to his own sense of himself as a person. Putting values into action, working hard for the best possible decisions, each individual is also contributing to the best outcomes for the community as a whole. Each worker-citizen knows that when the whole firm fares well, individual stakeholders will flourish too.

When people are treated to freedom, equality, and security, when they know that they are indeed the organization, when they believe passionately in the goodness of belonging to that organization, and when they take an active hand in steering justice and decision making through well-understood institutional processes, their organization will be capable of achieving truly astounding performance.

Capable indeed, but to sustain a record of outstanding accomplishment in an ever-changing and always-challenging competitive environment, a company of citizens must go beyond passionately translating values into structures, and vice versa, in moments of crisis. It must also repeatedly learn and support the behaviors of "doing citizenship." Values must be understood through civic practice, and civic practice must guide the operations and ongoing development of institutions. The system of citizenship requires the "secret sauce" of the third element of the triad, the day-to-day practices through which every citizen learns, as the Athenians did, the "how" of *politeia*. We turn to these all-important practices in our next chapter.

CHAPTER 5

Practicing Citizenship

PARTICIPATORY PRACTICES of citizenship were the single most important governance discovery of the ancient Athenians, and they offer a fundamentally important lesson for today's manager: Participatory practices are where citizenship *happens*. They are a kind of "secret sauce" because without explicit attention to practices, a citizen-centered organizational solution will remain little more than another cookbook recipe. Practices embody the combination of "doing" and "learning"—things that modern managers still tend to keep in separate jars. Most leaders of today's organizations grasp the importance of values and structures, but all too often they radically underappreciate the role of practices. Yet in the absence of robust participatory practices, an organization's effort to establish values and structures of self-governance is likely to be hollow and prone to failure. It is through practices that organizational citizenship is built, learned, and continuously improved.

When we speak of practices, we follow the Athenians in combining "doing citizenship" with "learning how to do it."

Like the physician who both engages in standard medical "practice" while "practicing" to become a better doctor, a citizen engages in governing his company and becomes better and more accomplished, both as a citizen and a person, in the process. Participatory practices embody knowledge, ways of behaving, ways of seeing problems and ideas, and, at the same time, an overall ethical stance. Practices mediate between values and structures by fostering the evolutionary shaping of values by structure— and the shaping of structure by values. Through the participatory practices, the values of individuality, community, and moral reciprocity are made manifest and actionable in the lives of individual citizens. Through the practices, the structures of governance become powerful tools for action and change by citizens. The practices are where the conviction that "the organization is an education for the betterment of each individual member" is transformed from a statement of mission to an actual schooling of citizens.[1]

We identify ten key practices of citizenship. Although they are grouped in four thematic categories, they are deeply interrelated. Their power lies in their "living reality," in the way they are embedded throughout the system of citizen-centered organizational self-governance.

PRACTICES OF ACCESS

The three practices (engagement, networks of networks, and rotation) that fall under the heading of access ensure that every citizen has a free and equal opportunity to participate in self-governance —taking part as an individual, team partner, or community member in the many processes of decision making, judgment, and execution that constitute the structure of governance. Yet the individual citizen does not expect to participate in all forums of governance all the time. He recognizes that his own good and the good of the community is best served when fellow citizens share among themselves the duties and privileges of governance, by "ruling and being ruled, in turns."

Engagement

The participatory practices begin with engagement—voluntary, spirited participation by individuals in the work and decisions of the community. The citizen's public identity is manifested by his or her engagement. Aristotle, with insightful economy of expression, said simply, "to be a citizen means participating in the Assembly and serving on juries."[2] The practice of engagement activates the value of community, the conviction that the people are the organization and vice versa. A feeling of engagement in the enterprise on the part of workers is, of course, something that any company strives for. Yet so many of today's workers are rightly cynical about the empty slogans of "being the most important asset" or "being the company." And indeed, such slogans will remain empty (and thus a source of cynicism rather than inspiration) unless workers have a real role in steering the organization through their active engagement, through participating as citizens in setting its policies, strategies, and the rules of justice.

Interesting questions arise when we view "engagement" within in the context of freedom, equality, and security—the three commitments that constitute the value of individuality. Engagement in the community as a source of "security" is clear enough: Rules are made and enforced by the democratic citizens themselves, for their own mutual protection. And "equality" is all about the equal right of every citizen to engage in the work of the community. But associating freedom with engagement may seem paradoxical: How can a citizen be really free to live as he chooses if he has a *duty* to engage in work, even if it is for the good of the community? The answer is that the company of citizens is based on managing often contradictory commitments, most fundamentally a loyalty both to one's self and to one's organization. The dynamic power of the citizen community is a product of the citizens' capacity to embrace and manage this paradox. Squaring a deep commitment to individual freedom with the practice of engagement in the community is a prime example of the citizen's art of "thinking alike while thinking differently."

Freedom and engagement are compatible in that a citizen (unlike an "asset") is free to choose to engage in steering the community to the extent of his ability. In modern parlance, he has a "positive right" to participate on equal footing with others.[3] In ancient Athens, this positive right of engagement was made real through economic incentives; citizens were reimbursed (with a modest but nontrivial payment to offset wages) to support their ability to spend time in decision making in the Assembly and Council, judgment in judicial settings, and execution as members of executive teams. This reimbursement was an important aspect of combining freedom with engagement: After all, it is meaningless to say that you are free to do something that you cannot possibly afford to do.

Yet, at the same time, each member of a company of citizens possesses a "negative right" as well: He is in fact free to spend time on his own projects, free *not* to volunteer for engagement in each and every facet of public decision making, judgment, and execution. In Athens there was no coercive or punitive enforcement of the right to participate in public business. In fact, most meetings of the national Assembly were not attended by more than about a quarter of the eligible citizen body. Similarly, of those who did attend, only a handful regularly spoke up, though many more made the choice to address their colleagues occasionally, when their special expertise was called for. We need to recognize that the duty to engage means only that each citizen will *periodically* be active in the governance of the organization. The good for each and all is not gained by every citizen's steady engagement in community decision making; it is gained by the shared recognition that each will take the opportunity to be engaged from time to time. Note also that the practice of engagement is about organizational governance, consistent with but separate from the work of earning one's own livelihood within the society. The value of freedom for Athenians did not imply a negative right to abstain from earning a living. Similarly, the practices of citizenship cannot flourish in a caretaker community populated by full-time bureaucrats or free riders. In a company of citizens, every citizen is expected contribute to the overall productivity of the organization as well as to its governance. In a company of citizens everyone recognizes that governance and productivity go together, and both demand the best efforts of each and every member.

The paradox of squaring "individual rights" and "duties owed to the community" is resolved by the "both/and" thinking that pervades the practice of engagement. As Pericles put it in his Funeral Oration (see chapter 2), Athenians were free to do as they like, but the citizen who *never* chose to participate in public affairs was disdained as "useless." "Duty" today often has the negative connotation of "taking your medicine"; but in a company of citizens engagement in the life of the organization is seen as exciting, honorable, and desirable for the expanded meaning it lends to individual lives.[4] Being expected to engage in the work of the community is not regarded as a burden, but as part of the good that comes with being a citizen. If you actually believe in what the community stands for, you certainly want to find a way to participate in shaping its destiny. Engagement affirms a higher organizational purpose and an extended sense of self. Pragmatically, it ensures that you have a hand in decisions that critically affect you.

In daily life, every Athenian (like every modern knowledge worker) was constantly choosing among competing demands on his time, labor, and knowledge. The Athenian delighted in public debates, although he could not always join them. Because citizens fundamentally trusted one another, it was unnecessary to be engaged all the time. The practice of engagement created an effective self-organizing process, which drew together many citizens only when big decisions had to be made, on a "just-in-time" basis. To mitigate the risk of subcritical mass, Athenians also established quorums so that a sufficient population always engaged in decisions of extraordinary consequence.[5]

Generally speaking, engagement ensures that each citizen has a genuine and action-based sense of ownership in the organization. It also helps to ensure that every decision benefits from the knowledge and inputs of a diverse body of people. As a consequence there is no need for a big "standing government" or complicated decision-making machinery. The company of citizens can make do with a few experts and "experienced amateurs," buttressed by practicing administrators, who carry out the day-to-day business of the organization on a rotating basis.

Networking Human Networks

The practice of networking human networks was discussed in detail in chapter 3, in the context of Cleisthenes' reforms. Manifest in both the designs of a company of citizens and many of its operations, the practice of networking assures access to positions of real responsibility for a broad cross section of the citizen body. Its goal is to foster innovation by building small subcommunities of trust, based on face-to-face interactions, then to combine and recombine these primary networks of citizens in different ways. New teams of citizens are constantly being built, but well-established relationships between people in working groups are leveraged by ensuring that these established groups can remain in meaningful contact with one another over the long run. In Athens, primary networks were established through the small (100- to 300-citizen) subcommunities of the demes (local villages and neighborhoods). Demes were the atomic level of governance for the Athenians, where families from regional neighborhoods governed themselves locally. But local governance never became parochial due to the mixing that took place at the national level. The Council of 500, as we saw in chapter 3, brought together councilors from several different parts of Athenian territory, but also kept groups of them productively together in the system of fifty-person "presidency teams." Citizens were variously kept together with their fellow deme-members and mixed with citizens from all parts of Athenian territory in other national institutions including the military, juries, and panels of executives.

The value of networking networks is already understood in many modern firms, which utilize cross-functional task forces, working groups, and teams. Much of the "democratizing" of modern companies began with the "team-based organization" of the 1980s, when managers began recognizing that more flexible, knowledge-intensive problem solving required combining the skills and experience of people from different domains in a common, performance-based working process. The ability of organizations to build, leverage, and combine "networks of networks" continues to accelerate, thanks to the Internet and new collaborative communications technology.

It is important, however, not to overemphasize the technology side of the networks story. The fundamental value found in electronic collaboration and communication is not the computer, software, or physical electronic networks themselves, but the knowledge and relationships built by engagement among their users.[6] And the most successful examples of networked people in modern organizations—whether it is a team, a community of practice, a collaborative alliance, or something similar—reflect a participative culture and experience for every member of the group.[7]

Scratch the surface of productive modern people networks and you're likely to find basic Athenian-style practices of citizen governance. Similarly, if one examines the reasons for the failure of networks or "knowledge communities," the cause is all too frequently an overreliance on technology as a substitute for human participation, combined with the lack of appropriate practices of engaged governance. Genuinely effective networks depend upon the development of a trust-based culture, and that kind of culture can only be built by people who have learned through practical experience the value (to individuals and communities) of exchanging knowledge, building on what other people know, and having an active hand in steering the direction of the work done together. Merely mandating or exhorting people to share what they know and to use what others know cannot create any sustainable organizational capability.[8]

Rotation

The third participatory practice of access, rotation, is the habit of taking turns at public service, both in positions of leadership and in the daily course of democratic decision making. "Taking turns" is closely related to the practice of engagement; it means that each citizen accepts that he will both "rule and be ruled" during his membership in the community. Most obviously, rotation is seen in the habit of speaking in turns during deliberative meetings; it is also seen in the selection of jurors for trials of justice by lot, and regular turnover in jury service. Rotation further means that, since a citizen's personal attendance at decision-making assemblies will not always be possible, he will trust others to take the job seriously, carrying out decisions in ways that factor in the needs and aspirations of diverse individuals.

Rotation among leadership will be familiar to anyone who has ever thought about the concept of "term limits." In a company of citizens one assumes that every office and position of authority will be temporary. In ancient Athens, officials were chosen by election or lottery, or some combination of the two (in general, the more critical the role, the more likely that the community would vote rather than choose by lot). But whatever the process of selection, all positions expired after a certain length of time (usually a year maximum), avoiding any kind of entrenched bureaucracy.[9] The bottom-line principle when implementing the practice of rotation must be that if a competent citizen wishes to serve his organization, he should have a chance to do so.

Rotation in leadership built on-the-job learning and experience throughout the citizen population. It supported the Athenian compromise between developing people and ensuring that the most capable were always in command, but also mitigated the risk that popular incompetents would hold sway for years on end. The practice further mitigated the risk of long-term incumbents abusing power or gaining extraordinary financial or political power in office. In addition, because so many Athenians had the experience of serving in a leadership position during their lifetimes, rotation also guaranteed that over time the community became collectively smarter and wiser, thus enhancing the development and sharing of knowledge intrinsic to a company of citizens. This is not to say that the Athenians never made serious mistakes, but it does help to explain why they were able to correct their missteps with resilient fortitude, rather than reacting to downturns with despair or panic.

PRACTICES OF PROCESS

Once access has been assured for all citizens, the practices associated with the process of governance (deliberation, transparency, and closure) come into play. Good process practices are essential if decision making, judgment, and execution are to be carried out in ways that are at once consistent, fair, and time-sensitive. Process practices establish both justice and effectiveness as central characteristics of the company of citizens.

Deliberation

The practice of deliberation means that the work of bodies responsible for decision making and judgment is predicated on consensus-seeking and mutual trust by well-intentioned members of the community. In contrast to a "winner-take-all" mentality that seeks to gain procedural victory, no matter how narrow, democratic decision making in the company of citizens is carried out in the belief that open discussions will typically identify the overall best answer; the role of the participants is to discuss matters in depth, pushing hard to discover the best answer through active mutual engagement.[10] The practice of deliberation is not about "warm and fuzzy" discussion intended to avoid hurting someone's feelings at all costs. It is intellectually rigorous, and can be hard-hitting, potentially even harsh. The Athenians developed the art of open debate to a high level; their assemblies and trials were battlegrounds of argument and counterargument. However, the battle was joined with everyone understanding that sharp debate led to better answers, and that discovering the best answer by the end of the day was in everyone's long-term interest.

The goal of deliberative practice is to find the best answer and push for a consensus that ensures optimal follow-through by everyone who has to live with the outcome. In Athens, the mechanics of voting reinforced such a goal. Although jury trials used secret ballots to guarantee fairness, Assembly decisions were usually determined by estimating the number of raised hands and getting a "sense of the meeting"; formal voting by ballots was employed only occasionally. The openness of the deliberative process helped each side in a debate understand the strength of feeling of the other. And because each citizen voted his conscience rather than a "party line," the alignment of voters changed from decision to decision.

In fact, "party line" is an anomalous concept in a company of citizens practicing deliberative process. Partisanship has no place in such a community. Notably the Athenians had no standing political parties—unlike modern representative democracies where party platforms are specifically designed to serve established interests.[11] In the company of citizens, groups will indeed form around critical decisions, and they will sometimes work aggressively to persuade fellow citizens of the wisdom of a certain course of action. But such groups do not become permanent factions. They are instead fluid and changeable, forming and dissolving according to changing circumstances and the critical issues to be decided, always centered on the goal of seeking the good of the overall community. In Athens, most citizens arrived at assemblies and trials with no preordained predisposition about how they would vote; they expected to be educated by the debate and to make their choices accordingly. Well-intentioned debate, guided by the practice of deliberation, was a cherished and critical part of the democratic system.

Deliberation does not imply a habit of inefficient discussion for its own sake or "group grope" on all possible topics. A common objection to democracy as a form of organization is that nothing gets done, given the tendency for everyone to endlessly debate about everything. The Athenian case shows that participatory democracy can be crisp and businesslike, even while remaining open and analytical. An important part of the practice of deliberation is the understanding that not all decisions need to be debated all the time by all citizens. In Athens, only the most important decisions were discussed in the largest assemblies. In a competitive environment, with external rivals and many demands on each citizen's time, there is no time for drawn-out debates about small things. However, when it really matters, and the stakes are high, citizens take the time to engage with one another to "unpack the truth." Ordinary matters are the responsibility of local decision-making groups and accountable executive teams. In Athens, demes, magistrates, and administrative leaders made thousands of decisions on their own every day.

Deliberation was not an Athenian monopoly; good examples of deliberative practices can be found in many organizations today. For example, well-run teams in any business setting typically practice some form of deliberation. When team members are goal-driven, with complementary skills, they enter into deliberative problem solving—trusting one another and believing everyone is trying to do the right thing for the overall project. They can disagree sharply and debate at length, but they know they do so in order to get to the best answer, not to undermine their colleagues. They know that not all decisions have to be made by the entire team, but also know that when it really matters to everyone's success, spending a little extra time working together to get a good answer and achieve consensus makes for the highest commitment in carrying through on decisions. This kind of decision making is pragmatic, fair, and motivating to participants.

Decision makers in a company of citizens understand that in reaching a decision, they are, in effect, giving orders to themselves. Their policy choices empower the relevant people or team to get the work done. In Athens, for example, when the citizens were discussing war and peace, they would bring their arms and armor to the Assembly. If the vote was for war, they expected to march out directly to the battlefield or to board the warships—acting on the orders they had given themselves. In a company of citizens, deliberation and action are intimately linked.

Transparency

The process practice of transparency supports deliberation and helps define the democratic culture of a company of citizens. In the context of deliberative decision making, transparency requires that all information relevant to policy making be available to the citizens evaluating any public question. In Athens, this meant that specialists in naval architecture were expected to speak up in matters of shipbuilding, and that witnesses with any knowledge of crimes should come forward in jury trials. Transparency also implies that the reasoning behind a decision—and indeed even arguments made to sway a final judgment—should be open, communicated, and understandable by the citizens. More broadly, transparency means that all social rules of the community—both laws and customs—should be clearly communicated and taught to all members. In a company of citizens, education in the rules governing behavior stresses not only the coercive—"don't do this"—but also the public welfare—"act this way, because it helps us all." Transparency as a process practice is a civic good.

Modern representative democracies, business firms, or other organizations may espouse a similar ethos of transparency—but in practical operation, leaders often obscure or hide the reasoning behind decisions from the members of the community. Specialized legal briefs, personal agendas, and behind-the-scenes lobbying undermine the sense that decisions and judgments affecting all members are made fairly, and thereby undermine the common commitment to action that is so essential to the organization's success. By contrast, a company of citizens insists on simplicity, openness, and trust; transparency encourages engaged follow-through for decisions taken on behalf of every member.

The Athenians deeply understood the importance of transparency. They kept the number of formal laws to a minimum. They used everyday language to explain both the substantive content of the laws and the legal processes used to apply the laws to individual cases. There was no specialized legal jargon in the ancient city. The Athenians completely avoided intermediation of lawyers or specialists in legal interpretation, and the rationale behind decisions in courts, assembly, and by administrators was freely available for all to hear and know.

The practice of transparency was central to the spirit of the Athenian culture. In his Funeral Oration, Pericles stressed the transparency of Athens: He proclaimed that the risk of damage from the high level of openness—the fear that enemies might discover the community's strategy—was outweighed by the good of everyone within the organization learning from everyone else.[12] Like deliberation, the practice of transparency is exemplified in modern organizations at the level of teams that manifest openness on all sides, so that everybody knows what's needed to get the job done, and when a decision is made, why it has been made. Transparency is fundamental to the creation of trust—which in recent years has been highlighted as critical to organizational performance.[13] But the Athenian case shows that trust is not so much an *input* to organizational design as a result of the practical *experience* of transparency. The practice of transparency enables decision making involving thousands of citizens, helps motivate them to engage in the process, and then encourages them to align themselves responsibly with its outcomes.

Closure

The practice of closure means that decisions are made and carried out in a time-sensitive fashion. It also means that all participants in the process agree to stand behind the decision once it has been made—whether a consensus has been reached or not. Even if a citizen voted against a proposal, closure means he is expected to support it in action (although he may challenge it in argument, as we explain below). The practice of closure is an important counterbalance to the tendency of democratic assemblies to debate matters at excessive length. In Athens, speeches by litigants in jury trials were limited in duration by a water clock. In the Assembly, major decisions were made in the course of a half-day meeting—the citizens had no time for pompous grandstanding or ill-informed blabbering that didn't move an issue forward. Athenians booed speakers from the podium when they wasted time by taking deliberations off course.[14] Closure did, however, allow for organizational flexibility as well as efficiency and speed; by practicing closure in the context of deliberation and transparency, the community found the middle ground between being resolute and remaining open to new opportunities. The Athenian experience of participatory decision making allowed for the will of the people to alter its course—especially if new facts or compelling opinions came forward.

One of the most famous cases of revisiting a decision occurred during the early years of the Peloponnesian War, after the Athenians suppressed a revolt by the subject city of Mytilene. At a meeting of the national Assembly, the citizens initially voted to execute all male Mytilenians, as a lesson to the rest of the empire. Following the vote, a warship was dispatched from Athens to Mytilene, ordering the executions. But in the course of numerous private discussions, it became clear that many citizens recognized that the vote had been taken in anger, and represented bad policy. A second meeting was called for the next day. After another vigorous debate, a second vote overturned the previous decision. A second ship was immediately sent out with the countermanding order, "Overtake the first ship and spare the Mytilenians!" It was a fast decision, followed by an equally quick change to a better policy, and so (thanks to athletic rowing by the crew of second ship) the Mytilenians were spared. This nimbleness was made possible by the capacity of the company of citizens to learn from their own successes and their own errors over time. In the Assembly, speakers often referenced earlier decisions—good and bad—in support of what they believed to be the right course; this appeal to history reflects the conviction that the organization should learn from past experience.[15] The concern for achieving closure must not stand in the way of new learning.

The experience of decision making employing the practices of deliberation, transparency, and closure teaches citizens to have faith in their own processes of judgment. It allows debate to be efficient, open, and gets everybody "on board" by the end of the day. At the same time, citizens feel empowered, but not compelled, to second-guess their own decisions from time to time. Because its processes of decision making are both nimble and open, the company of citizens can be comfortable with occasionally changing course.

PRACTICES OF CONSEQUENCE

Access ensures that the right people will be involved in decision making, judgment, and execution; process ensures that decisions are made fairly so that they gain the acceptance of the entire community. But the success of the company of citizens also depends on a general recognition that actions have consequences. The consequences of actions can be positive or negative, and the company of citizens must be very clear-eyed about both possibilities, rewarding and censuring accordingly. Paying attention to consequence means ensuring that merit is honored, that those who propose policy and carry it out are accountable for their work, and that misconduct and poor decisions are promptly challenged. Three practices frame the notion of consequence in a company of citizens: merit-based decision making, accountability, and challenge.

Merit

The practice of recognizing merit means that decisions are based on the best case put forward; excellence, not position, prejudice, or privilege, is the criterion for choice. In a company of citizens, the best case for action is that which carries the day after open, sufficient, and informed debate. Merit means that every thoughtful and knowledgeable individual, with good ideas based on real understanding, will get a hearing. The incompetent blowhard will not. The practice of merit gives lie to the idea that participatory democracy must devolve to the lowest common denominator.

A company of citizens recognizes that good decisions must be made, because the judgments materially affect each and every citizen by demanding committed action. Citizens understand that if good decisions are to be made promptly, and the attention of a large body of participants is to be engaged in making those decisions, then the people expressing opinions in public have to know what they are talking about. And if they don't, they should not get much of a hearing. In Athens, the market of public opinion was tough but even-handed in its judgments. Even Demosthenes, who eventually became a highly respected leader, was laughed off the podium in his earliest attempts to address the Assembly. It was only after he learned to speak with precision on matters that he had fully mastered that he was able to gain and keep the attention of the assembled citizenry.[16]

Merit coupled with the commitment to equality promotes the rise and development of excellence, regardless of one's connections or lack thereof. The renowned Athenian diplomat and public speaker, Aeschines, for example, began life as the son of an impoverished schoolteacher. He later worked as a clerk in the public offices and after that was an actor in the Athenian theater. He rose to a position as a diplomat and eventually became a renowned and honored civic leader. He did so on the basis of talent and experience gained and demonstrated before his peers. He proved that he had the ability to clearly express issues about which he had substantial knowledge. Athenian history is filled with examples of socially disadvantaged citizens going on to great glory on the basis of excellence in their democratic and professional careers.[17]

The community practiced merit and exemplified it through those that rose to positions of leadership. By the same token, the Athenians always remained highly critical of leaders' performance. Even the most well-established political speaker would quickly lose his capacity to command the audience's attention if he began talking on affairs about which he knew little or had little experience, or if he were caught misrepresenting the relevant facts. Reputations in a democratic community are results-driven; yesterday's hero can find himself ignored if he fails to reach today's expected goals. In Athens, even famous leaders such as Pericles were reprimanded for failures in judgment or execution.

The Athenian practice of merit shaped the political community as an overall leadership school. With thousands of citizens continually gaining practical experience in public affairs and the processes of governance, the Athenian company of citizens acted as a vast engine of leadership development. The experience of playing a leadership role, available to so many citizens of diverse backgrounds, ensured that individuals could grow and expand their responsibilities in the future through experience. Similarly, for every failure, there was a successor waiting in the wings, ready to step in and take charge of any needed public office, project, or campaign. In the Assembly, after a bad idea was shouted down, fresh and willing voices were raised with new proposals. The practice of honoring merit meant that a ready supply of the best ideas and talented people would continue to rise to the top.

Accountability

Accountability is a vitally important practice in a company of citizens. In its most basic form, it touches every citizen—everyone is held accountable by everyone else to respect the values of individuality, to work for the good of the community, and to obey the common rules. Accountability is evident throughout the processes of decision making, and is particularly relevant to the conditions and performance of any kind of leadership. In the forums of decision making, all citizens are accountable for the quality and value of the ideas they express. Good ideas are praised. In Athens, successful proposers of new policies were honored by having their name attached to the public decree, and carved in stone when the decree was posted in the public square. On the other hand, those who sponsored bad legislation might be sued in court on the grounds that their suggestions were dangerous, misleading, or destructive.

The process of public judgment tested individual policies for alignment with the broader values of the community. As a consequence, skilled speakers, who might have been tempted to play on people's emotions in order to pass a dangerous policy, were forced to think twice; leaders needed to pay careful attention, not only to whether they could successfully get a measure through the Assembly, but to how that policy would hold up in the long run. Accountability encouraged voluntary self-control and thus curbed the dangers of demagoguery. Those who willfully misled the community would pay the price.

That's very different than much of the rhetoric of today's "learning organization." We often hear how such entities must create a risk-free culture, where people are allowed to fail without penalty. The modern leader faces a dilemma: How to balance "no-fault" with the consequences of bad performance? The Athenians saw no paradox at work in their practice of accountability. They insisted on accountability for performance as part of the overall learning process; the "safety net" was not a "no-blame" ethic, but rather the sense of fairness in a large community of citizens who were capable of judging the significance of mistakes.

Not every misstep was prosecuted, and being a leader meant being able to take public criticism. Leaders could also rely on the buffering effect of the "law of large numbers" (that is, a plenitude of opinions tends to converge around a reasonable middle ground) and on their understanding of community values as the benchmark for what was likely to be judged to be right or wrong. Nonetheless, more than a few Athenian leaders had to defend themselves—not always successfully—against charges arising from a perceived failure in their public service. And "public service" could be construed quite broadly. In one of the most famous legal cases in Athenian history, the philosopher Socrates was held accountable—and ultimately sentenced to death—for public actions that were regarded by his peers as dangerous to the overall community. We will look at this remarkable case in more detail at the end of this chapter.

In Athens, all appointed, elected, or allotted leaders—at all levels—were accountable to the community, both before and after taking office. Before taking office, leaders had to undergo a public scrutiny of their background, past behavior, and character. After their job or project was complete, they had to go again before a panel of citizens for judgment of the work done. These post-performance panels investigated whether office-holders had engaged in corruption or misuse of public monies, or more generally acted in ways counter to the overall interest of the community. But the stakes for leader performance in Athens were not merely about escaping censure. Because of the intense focus on service to the community and the honor that accompanied public service, leaders also felt accountability to fellow members in emotional and intangible ways. The same will be true in any company of citizens. Success offers a chance to shine brightly, to be honored by genuine equals for genuine accomplishments. The collective judgment of peers plays a powerful role, not only in "holding people's feet to the fire," but also in stimulating the voluntary will to achieve excellence. It encourages every would-be leader to strive to gain recognition, and presses every established leader to demonstrate that he genuinely merits ongoing public acclaim and responsibility.

Challenge

The third practice of consequence is challenge—the right to seek to reverse misguided policy or decisions or to call attention to misbehavior. Challenge is an essential complement and counterbalance to the other participatory practices. Challenge has several instantiations: In the most familiar to us living in modern Western democracies, it is the right to appeal a judgment, as the Athenians did when they appealed a magistrate's judgment to the whole community sitting as a jury. Decisions of the Assembly could also be challenged and overturned, as we already saw in the example of the debate following the revolt of Mytilene.

But challenge also takes many other forms in the company of citizens. It includes the kind of "gadfly" role played by Socrates in his life as a questioning public philosopher: calling upon one's fellow citizens to be more self-critical and more aware of the consequences of their everyday patterns of thought and behavior. More generally, challenge means the sense that every citizen is responsible for the welfare of every other—that each should call attention to mistreatment of individuals within the organization, even if that mistreatment has no immediate bearing on one's own life. It means blowing the whistle on misdeeds that harm the good of the community, or that compromise its fundamental values. In Athens, each citizen had the right—and duty—to prosecute another citizen or public official whose actions, behavior, or proposals were injurious to the community, or were misaligned with the values of the organization.

The right to challenge also meant that every Athenian had recourse if and when he was mistreated—if he were insulted or harmed by an aberrant individual or bullied by a public official. For the Athenians, the practice of challenge protected each citizen's basic dignity. It guaranteed that the values of individuality, community, and moral reciprocity would remain real and practical, rather than devolving into empty rhetoric in some quickly forgotten code of organizational ethics or high-minded mission statement. Righting a private wrong always implied also righting a public wrong on behalf of the community.

An incident involving the orator Demosthenes illustrates how the practice of challenge worked to protect the individual and the community alike.[18] One day, during his service in an important public role, Demosthenes was attacked and slapped in the face by a powerful political enemy. Moreover, the incident occurred before the entire citizen body, in the great public theater in the center of the city. Demosthenes went before a court and demanded that his adversary, a certain Meidias, be punished. Demosthenes did not claim that the slap had done him any physical harm; rather, he argued that the blow was an insult to him as a citizen, and therefore to the free, equal, and secure standing of each individual citizen and thus of the entire community. His speech to the hundreds of his fellow citizens sitting in judgment equated the arrogance of a man whom he freely admitted was his private enemy with a threat to the democratic system as a whole. If the dignity of any one citizen—especially one fulfilling a public duty—could be assaulted at will, he argued, then each citizen was at risk. The vital security of the individual could not survive the willingness of the community to let this sort of slight go unpunished. Demosthenes' challenge to a private wrong had a public purpose: to restore the proper balance of behavior in society. Demosthenes won his case, and the recognition he gained in this and other prominent challenges of misconduct helped to build his reputation as a community-minded leader.

Demosthenes, like other public speakers in Athens, reminded his audience that public judgments and the punishment of wrongdoers were essential parts of the education of every citizen. Remedies were not merely revenge; they instructed members of the community how it was and was not appropriate to act. We can contrast the Athenian approach to the participatory practices with modern corporate processes in which wrongs are handled discretely, out of sight, often in the "black box" of Human Resources. The obsessive concern of organizations today with legal liabilities and also for protecting feelings can undermine valuable opportunities to "teach and learn by example," and to affirm norms of the community that bind citizens together and align them with a common sense of purpose and mutual responsibility.

JURISDICTION: DECIDING APPROPRIATE ACTION IN THE RIGHT PLACE

The nine practices falling under the headings of access, process, and consequence are each subject to the discipline of an essential tenth practice—jurisdiction. The work of "doing citizenship" will not succeed in either its practical or educational roles if it is not done at the right place and at the right time. The practice of jurisdiction—meaning that the appropriate people take responsibility for deciding and carrying out appropriate actions at the right time and in the right place within the organization—is vital to the effective operation of the system of participatory citizenship. Jurisdiction helps to answer the complex and all-important question: "What decisions belong to whom and where should they be made?" Jurisdiction in a company of citizens pushes decision making as close as possible to where the decision actually takes effect, and to those people on whom the obligation of accountability most properly falls. By the same token, it is through practicing jurisdiction that decision-making bodies are kept appropriate in composition and size to the scope and impact of the decisions' effects.

In Athens, jurisdiction as a practice is illustrated by the example of granting citizenship itself—of conferring membership in the community. In the democratic city, the decision of whether or not to confirm an individual as an Athenian citizen was pushed down to the local level. It was made in an open assembly, by the citizens of the home deme—by neighbors, men who had reason to know the background, character, and virtues of the candidate. Although the official rule was that only sons of Athenian fathers and mothers could be confirmed as citizens by decision of a deme assembly, your neighbors might well decide to overlook a bit of uncertainty about your actual ancestry so long as your character merited inclusion in the body of citizens. On the other hand, the decision to grant official citizenship to someone who was clearly a foreigner was regarded as a matter that affected all Athenians. Each officially naturalized citizen brought something new to the community as a whole. That could be a great benefit to the city-state, but it also entailed significant risk—the Athenians were cautious about anything that might "dilute" their core identity. Membership in the community was a deadly serious decision. So, following the practice of jurisdiction, this very important matter was always put to the whole body of Athenians. Naturalization of foreigners was decided by the national Assembly open to all existing citizens, and required a full quorum in attendance.[19]

In the modern, hierarchical organization, there is always tension about how much the "corporate center" versus a geographical or business unit should control and decide. The Athenians in their demes and villages didn't waste time worrying about intrusion of the central authority into local affairs; after all, through the practice of networked networks, they were themselves both the centralized and decentralized authority at the same time. In matters of governance, Athenians participated both locally and nationally, and their "corporate center" was thus distributed and virtual as well as physical and central. Decision making thus could be built from the "bottom up" as well as from the "top down." The Athenians reserved many matters for local decision making, moving matters up to the central institutions of the Assembly and courts only when it was something that affected the welfare of the entire community. For example, decisions about war and peace always went to the national Assembly; decisions about local festivals stayed in the demes. Jury courts open to all mature Athenians tried capital crimes; individual arbitrators or regional magistrates handled minor or local infractions.

Jurisdiction is a distinguishing practice of the modern U.S. system of federal courts. Comparing and contrasting the federal court system to jurisdiction in a company of citizens is instructive. Most U.S. federal case judgments are made locally (in district courts); the Supreme Court only gets involved in a case when an important general principle is at stake. The Supreme

Court refuses to hear many cases, allowing judgments of lower courts to stand as decided. As in a company of citizens, these processes help shape a distributed and efficient model. But in the U.S. federal system, the modern governmental principle of "separation of powers" tends to minimize shared learning and experience: The architecture of decision making ensures that the people sitting on the Supreme Court are not the same people who sit on the local courts, nor do any of them also serve in the executive or legislative branches of government. Therefore, much "cross-boundary" negotiation takes place, framed by a concern to maintain checks and balances.

Those trade-offs make sense in a modern constitutional government. But they are unnecessary in a company of citizens who trust one another, based on shared practices, learning, and values. Athenian decision making—legislative, judicial, and executive—involved all the same people, participating equally in all processes and at all levels. For the Athenians, decision making was flexible and dynamic, embracing more or less of the whole community, and changeable as the need and stakes dictated. Jurisdiction in Athens took advantage of scalability as part of its concern with appropriateness of personnel and location. Athenian decisions could move and expand, both horizontally and vertically, to include those most affected by the decision itself. Over time and through constant practice, the community continuously refined its own collective sense of where and to whom decisions most rightly belonged.

DOING AND LEARNING

Through practicing Athenian-style citizenship, people learn that self-governance is an actionable, behavioral, and educational imperative for every member of a community. The lessons of practice, however, are not always easy. Turning once again to history, let's look at a famous case that illustrates the centrality of practices to the life of the individual citizen: The dramatic story of the trial and execution of Socrates, Athens' most famous philosopher, in 399 B.C.

Several years before the trial, certain Athenians, claiming to be Socrates' students, had turned traitor and had gone on to lead the oligarchic reign of terror in the city after the Peloponnesian War. After the restoration of democracy, Socrates was convicted on charges of having "corrupted the youth" and, through apparent implication because of his supposed students' treasonous actions, was found guilty and sentenced to death. While he was awaiting execution, some of Socrates' friends offered to smuggle him out of prison and across the border. But Socrates spurned their offer, explaining that he had lived his whole life in Athens and that now it was his duty to accept the legal judgment of the citizens. Socrates believed himself to be innocent, a judgment endorsed by most modern audiences looking back at the case. But at the time Socrates drew a sharp distinction between the human error of practical judgment made by the jurors who convicted him and the fairness of the overall system of governance. Socrates pointed out to his friends that he had personally benefited from his Athenian upbringing and education in Athenian laws and customs; now he refused to "harm the laws" by breaking them in a prison escape. And so he drank the hemlock and died.

The education that Socrates had received in his life as a citizen, and ultimately died to uphold, was explicit in the practices we described above. Socrates made his most important civic contribution as a critical gadfly in the public square, seeking to improve his fellows by tirelessly challenging them to critically examine their own values. He sharply reprimanded his fellow citizens when they deviated from their own established procedures of justice. But, in common with other citizens, Socrates also attended the Assembly, listening carefully to debates on public matters and voting for the best policy. He served as an infantryman in the Athenian army, accepting orders from the elected generals. He served a year on the Council of 500, where he worked on a tribal team of fifty, set agendas for the Assembly, met foreign ambassadors, and otherwise looked after public business.

As a citizen, Socrates learned, through the practices of participation, how to judge arguments, obey orders, and work cooperatively on networked teams. He learned how to rule and how to be ruled in his turn. And he learned how to challenge his fellow citizens when he believed they were doing something wrong. Finally, he learned to accept full responsibility for his actions, and he willingly accepted the judgment of his community when it affected him personally—even when he believed that the judgment was in error. Socrates was an exceptional person in many ways, but he died, as he had lived, as simply an engaged citizen of his democratic community.[20]

The tale of Socrates shows us not only that citizens sometimes make mistakes in judgment, but also that "practice(s) make perfect"—or at least that participatory practices, systematically pursued, lead to better self-governance over time. It is clear enough, in hindsight, that the Athenian democracy in 399 B.C. made a grave mistake in putting its most famous and dedicated gadfly to death. Socrates was found guilty of charges that included "corrupting the youth," but he clearly had corrupted no one. His fierce interrogations of those willing to talk with him in the public square only helped people start on the hard path of "knowing themselves." Socrates regarded challenging people's

entrenched habits of thinking as his mission as a democratic citizen. It is unfortunate that in the context of a particular moment
in Athens' history, a majority of his peers disagreed.

History shows that, here as elsewhere in a democratic society,
thousands of citizens talking and voting together can still make
faulty judgments. But through the engagement and experience
that comes from practicing self-governance, the best companies
of citizens will improve and self-correct over time. Socrates'
death was not in vain; his fellow citizens learned from their mistake and never again brought such legal charges against a philosopher. Critical philosophy flourished in Athens in the century
after Socrates' death. Athenian history is far from an unbroken
record of right judgments, but mistaken judgments like the conviction of Socrates were typically followed by stronger and better decision making thereafter. This happens because practices
seamlessly combine the excitement and experience of "doing it
in real time" with learning and building experience through
one's life.

The participatory practices of citizenship are where, in a
democratic community, common-sense views of "how things *are*
done around here" meet with the values and aspirational principles of "how things *ought* to be done around here." As a set of
both behaviors and behavioral expectations, practices manifest
the underlying logic of just and fair processes of self-governance.
They are reflected by and embedded in the governance structures and they give life and animation to the values of citizenship.
Participatory practices were first developed in ancient Athens,
but they are equally identifiable in today's company of citizens.

Indeed, each of the ten participatory practices discussed in
this chapter can be seen in the operational routines of many of
today's innovative and forward-looking organizations. In workplace

teams, virtual communities, or companies with participative or open book management, one can find members practicing and defending behaviors and ways of "seeing and doing," such as engagement, rotation, merit, challenge, accountability, and the like.[21] We would argue, however, that there are three important differences between most examples of modern "participative management" and what the Athenians originally discovered and practiced.

First, although modern companies or other organizational units sometimes do pursue some of these participatory practices, rarely do they do so with the same self-conscious explicitness that the Athenians manifested. When practices remain only implicit, the power of democratic thinking, learning, and commitment among members of the community remains less than it could be.

Second, although participatory practices do exist in modern organizations, it is still uncommon to find all of them in place and working together, in the kind of holistic system that the Athenians found to be so powerful and self-sustaining. To truly work as the company of citizens' "secret sauce," all ten ingredients of practice need to become part of the way an organization governs itself.

Finally, modern organizations' experiments with participative management systems have not reached for the scale and ambition of Athenian democracy—where some thirty thousand citizens year in and year out practiced citizenship and made decisions on behalf of themselves and the community at large.

The differences between the Athenian experience and the experiments of modern organizations stand as opportunities to reinvent the future in light of the lessons of a very special past. By focusing on the gap between the ancient model and modern practice, we can consider the implications of the Athenian model for the world of today's knowledge economy—a world that is in some ways very different than anything previously known, but in other ways surprisingly familiar. Our concluding chapter tackles this challenge.

CHAPTER **6**

Building Today's
Company of Citizens

TWO CENTURIES after the democratic Athenian Revolution of 508 B.C. and the establishment of a company of citizens by the reforms of Cleisthenes, the glorious Parthenon was put to a new and peculiar use. A Macedonian king, Demetrius the Besieger, persuaded the Athenians to make him a citizen of their polis, and then he promptly claimed the famous temple as his private palace. The Athenians had no real choice about accepting Demetrius' bear hug takeover; his large and proficient army had occupied the city and he was already its true master. Athens' glory days and the era of leaders such as Themistocles, Pericles, and Demosthenes were over.

Demetrius' conquest of the city capped a generation that had witnessed the astounding rise of Macedon (in northern Greece) under Philip II and Alexander the Great. By the time Demetrius settled into his impressive new Athenian residence, the power equation in the Greek world had changed for good. Macedonian armies had conquered all of Greece and then had gone on to overthrow the Persian empire to the east. Vast stores of gold and silver, accumulated through centuries of careful Persian adminis- tration, flooded the markets of the Greek world, altering beyond recognition the established structures of economic and political power. The Greek city-states were now pawns in the strategic plans of Macedonian generals who competed against one an- other for power in the aftermath of the death of Alexander the Great. Although the Athenians would try to reassert independ- ence for years to come, their freedom and preeminence as a lead- ing Greek power was permanently lost. Their Macedonian rulers were eventually succeeded by the next great conquerors, the Ro- mans. Under their regime, Athens assumed the role that would be its long-term destiny: a cultured university town within some- one else's great empire. The Athenians' fall from their former position of power had a simple cause: Their company of citizens was overwhelmed by the superior military power of the Mace- donians and the Romans.[1]

The eventual transformation of Athens from a vital and inno- vative company of citizens to a quiet university town raises fun- damental questions for any leader seeking lessons to apply to the modern enterprise. Was the fall of Athens inevitable? If so, does that mean that the citizen-centered model is not viable in the long term? If the Athenians' fall from power was not inevitable, what could they have done differently that would have allowed the city to continue to prosper as a free, creative, powerful, and high-performing community? In either case, what are the most important lessons learned and implications for leaders thinking about how to build a contemporary company of citizens?

In answer to the first question, we resist the notion that any failure is inevitable, nor do we agree with those who assert that every human enterprise is eventually destined to die. Any good manager knows that organizational success and failure depends on many factors, including timing, planning, talent, and the quality of thinking behind hard managerial choices. It's never simply a matter of luck or fate. For the Athenian company of citizens, the long and remarkable, if not always easy, ride as a leading organization was largely due to its distinctive culture of self-governance.[2] This dynamic system of democratic values, structures, and participatory practices remains a timeless and durable paradigm of human organization; indeed versions of it are visible in any number of successful modern organizations, communities, teams, and working groups.[3]

The model served the Athenians well for two hundred years. It would have continued to serve them well, but only if they had extended and adapted it through their continuing history. The Athenians finally lost out to other great empires because they failed to find ways to allow the true power of the citizen community to continuously evolve. In order to resist the Macedonians and Romans, the Athenians would have had to expand the capacity of the overall organization while preserving its culture, specifically enlisting more people as citizens, while also extending fuller rights and responsibilities to others. How might they have gone about doing that?

In the most basic analysis, the Athenian *politeia* was "outgunned" by the large militaristic systems of Macedon and Rome. The company of citizens was incapable of matching the human and material resources commanded by these great empires. But perhaps it didn't have to be that way. Suppose the Athenians had extended their citizen-centric system to a much broader population, building up their own large reserves of committed people and military potential. As we have seen, Athenian citizenship was ordinarily limited to native adult males. But

Athenian society also included potentially valuable human capability above and beyond the limited group of people who were full citizens: women, slaves, resident foreigners, and even imperial subjects. Many individuals among these noncitizen groups had actually proved remarkably loyal to Athens in times of crisis— risking their fortunes and even their lives for the sake of the democratic *politeia*. Yet with only limited exceptions (for example Pasion, the freed slave whose successful career was discussed in chapter 2), Athenian citizenship remained a jealously guarded privilege of native-born men. Moreover, the city had a range of relationships with other city-organizations, whose people could also have been resources in the struggles against the great empires. Taken together, the noncitizen population linked to Athens was substantial.

Why did the Athenians miss this opportunity? Why did they disobey the fundamental logic of their own democratic principles, which stressed freedom, equality, human potential, and the virtue of participation in the community?

Two barriers—one practical, the other cultural—led to the Athenians' undoing. First, the democratic system ran up against physical limitations. The system was founded on the premise that any citizen could personally attend and participate, face-to-face, in deliberations at any public meeting. Therefore, given the limited capacity of the unamplified human voice, public spaces for civic participation were unable to handle more than several thousand deliberating citizens at any one time. Without modern interactive communications technology, Athenians could not even begin to consider involving hundreds of thousands of people in decision-making processes. The implicit duty to be present in person, coupled with limitations on space and coordination of public meetings, significantly bounded the Athenians' ability to include vastly more people in processes of self-governance.

Yet the cultural barrier to expanding the membership of the Athenian company of citizens weighs even more heavily. Although the Athenians transcended many of the cultural assumptions of their age, when it came to citizenship they were actually quite conservative. The original democratic revolution had substantially expanded the membership in the organization. But after the revolution the Athenians followed a set of social norms that our contemporary judgments would hold to be xenophobic and sexist. The idea of extending citizenship well beyond the circle of native-born males was raised by visionary social critics but never adopted. What now appears to be a profound cultural blindness on the part of the ancient citizens undermined the ability of the Athenian community to embrace and align the much greater source of knowledge and labor that might have enabled them to compete with the powerful and hierarchical empires of Macedon and Rome.

ORGANIZATIONAL CITIZENSHIP TODAY

Today's organizations do not have to make the same trade-offs. Modern leaders are subject to neither the practical nor the cultural barriers that limited the Athenians' performance capacity as a company of citizens in the age of ancient empires. And therefore, the historical fate of Athens is no impediment to implementing citizen-centered solutions today. To the contrary, we argue that today's enterprises have both the need and the opportunity to build cultures and systems of participatory governance in the spirit of the Athenian model. The *need* for citizenship is the imperative of organizations to achieve ever higher levels of innovation and performance in an era of increasing dependence on people and what they know—people who want to be free and equal and who demand a role in steering their own destiny.

The citizen-centered solution links that need to an *opportunity:* Most of today's workers are already familiar with many of the values and structures of democracy. Leaders today can expect a diverse range of people will be capable of making a substantial contribution and therefore deserve "rights of participation." Unlike the Athenians, we no longer exclude people from the chance of citizenship on the basis of gender or nonnative origin. That political openness can be tapped—and extended—in the processes of modern companies. Most organizations today already have some experience with people sharing knowledge for the good of their team or business unit, debating ideas for the best solution, appealing to merit for decisions, sharing leadership responsibilities, challenging bad judgments, and operating through informal networks of networks. Beneath the surface, almost all organizations are to some degree self-governing; it is a natural consequence of the progressive "flattening" of enterprises that we have witnessed for the past thirty years. Moreover, the growing promise of communications technology to facilitate collaborative relationships across time and space potentially make democratic solutions more feasible across wide geography and large populations.

Taken together, experience with democracy, a socially inclusive mind-set, the flattening of organizational hierarchies, and the explosion of modern technology would seem to bias today's organizations toward adopting a company of citizens solution. More equality in the workplace for women, minorities, and immigrants has expanded the modern workforce. By taking the steps necessary to create a self-governing culture, organizations should thrive with the greater pool of talented people eager to take on a larger role in governing their own work communities. And advanced technologies that enable virtual meetings, decision making, and large-group communication would seem to promise an almost limitless ability to enable self-governance for hundreds of thousands or even millions of people.

At this point, however, the story becomes more complicated. Although the unique conditions of modernity offer unprecedented need and opportunity for citizen-style companies, those same conditions also pose unprecedented challenges for organizational self-governance. The global economy, technological change, demographic shifts, and a host of other forces affecting modern enterprises have had the effect of blurring distinctions between private lives and commercial life, have undone traditional notions of job security and commitment, and have opened up marketplaces for talent and labor more fluid than ever before.[4] The conditions of the new global economy have also put more power into the hands of institutional investors, who own millions of shares in public companies and who are not hesitant to use their holdings to exert influence on organizational management.[5] Moreover, in a world of free agents, outsourcing, temporary and part-time workers, demanding shareholders, and organizations that regularly expand and contract, concepts of membership, ownership, commitment, and accountability are complex and highly changeable. Building a company of citizens therefore becomes a more nuanced and challenging process. The task goes well beyond simply empowering a broad membership within a relatively stable community and beyond encouraging participatory practices among committed members of a unitary enterprise.

By the same token, the promise of new communications technology to accelerate and extend the opportunity for citizen-style participation and engagement in organizations will not be fulfilled without careful attention to people as social beings. The advent of global e-mail, teleconferencing, and Internet-enabled collaborative tools has progressively expanded our horizons for building and sustaining communities across time and space. But for all the enthusiasm about "virtuality," face-to-face interaction remains vitally important in creating strong working relationships. The Athenians knew that the passion and engagement of people debating and making decisions in person are critical components of a company of citizens. Some of today's visionaries predict a quick and seamless transformation to an era of widespread participation in political deliberations; they imagine some kind of gigantic national "teledemocracy."[6] But it's not yet proven that the application of new technologies, in and of themselves, could ever completely replace the human dimension of personal interaction. It seems certain that technological advances will continue to redefine the potential of business organizations to function as communities and will increase the potential for large-scale distributed self-governance. Yet we simply don't have enough experience at this point to predict how big participatory and self-governing human communities can grow, while still remaining engaged, morally reciprocal, and devoted to ongoing learning.[7]

THE ARCHITECTURE OF CITIZENSHIP

Leaders who have read this far and who have recognized both the pressing need and the exciting opportunities to build a company of citizens today will also understand that the revolutionary/evolutionary process of implementation cannot come in the form of a simple top-down mandate or exhortation to follow a simple blueprint. The building process must include the potential "citizen-members" who will help create and will come to live the values of the community. Furthermore, as the examples of Cleisthenes and Pericles demonstrate, leadership is essential in design, example, and inspiration. Just as building the Parthenon required leaders who understood the architecture of marble temples, building a company of citizens requires leaders who understand the "architecture of citizenship." That is, it requires leaders who grasp the foundational principles of citizenship explained in this book—yet who also understand that these principles will be need to be applied pragmatically in the unique setting of their own companies and business challenges.

Taking a leading role in building a company of citizens means thoughtfully applying citizenship principles to a specific organizational context. That means leading in helping people make good "design choices" based on several key variables (discussed below). It means paying attention to what happens when those choices are put into practice. Grasping the architecture of citizenship, like citizenship itself, is all about implementing the practice of "learning while doing." It involves continuously learning from the company's developing experience of self-governance, integrating the outcomes of design choices into what the company knows, and building on that learning to create a dynamic system of values and structure.

The development of each company's distinctive architecture of citizenship will be framed by the six variables of purpose, fit, size, membership, leadership, and organizational maturity. Let's examine each of these in turn. The first three variables apply to all organizations, whatever their governance structure, and can be addressed quite succinctly. The last three lie at the heart of the solution to the "entrepreneurial individual/focused community paradox" that we offer in this book; that is, how to create organizations that both respect the autonomy and drive of each person while also aligning their collective effort for maximum scale impact. In each section we pose questions that leaders will want to ask themselves as they begin designing and implementing an architecture of citizenship for their own organizations.

Purpose

The first variable, purpose, requires developing a shared understanding among the citizens-to-be about the mission and goals of the community. Does the organization have a clear sense of its own mission and goals? Are they respected by its members? Does the brand of the organization reflect meaning for its members as well as for its clients? As we have stressed repeatedly, mission and goals will always imply some kind of performance challenge to the collective members—that is, to meet their mission and goals, the community must accomplish specific outcomes and results. Mission and goals may be as diverse as achieving superior client service while also developing people, pioneering innovation by creating distinctive products in a particularly competitive market, creating wealth while still remaining independent in the face of corporate takeover, or lessening suffering by reaching starving children with a new nutritional program. Each case will have corresponding and specific performance imperatives. Building a company of citizens to achieve these will mean believing that those imperatives, and the mission and goals they support, will be better reached by collective effort and empowered action.

Fit

Fit is a critical variable reflecting the appropriateness and alignment of the organizational model to the needs of the corporation and the abilities of its people. Are the organization's people ready to grow into the role of citizens, and does a citizen model make sense for what the company is trying to accomplish? The company of citizens model is not a "one-size-fits-all" solution and will never be universally adopted. No organizational model in itself guarantees long-term success, and different business needs will call for different ways of organizing. The vast and complex ecosystem that is the world of work in the global economy will continue to support different approaches to creating value. Plenty of hierarchically organized companies thrive today, and others will continue to rise—even as others fall—in the future.

That said, we believe that the company of citizens model is an increasingly appropriate solution to at least some of today's most pressing challenges, and it could successfully be applied to a range of different business and organizational situations. On the surface, the easiest fit between a self-governing citizenship model and an actual firm might seem to be the case of organizations that are knowledge-intensive, made up of professionals who are autonomous in terms of what they know and what they do, and collaborative in terms of their need to solve increasingly complex problems. Thus consulting, accounting, advertising, engineering, scientific or research firms, or any of a host of not-for-profit organizations provide examples of a potential "good fit."

But there are also many cases of participative management already existing in manufacturing firms. These experiences demonstrate that citizenship can be a highly effective way of organizing workers who have to depend on one another in complex, capital- and process-intensive businesses. They help point the way to creating fully realized companies of citizens in a wide variety of business enterprises.[8] In the end, the critical decisions that must be made in regard to fit are not so much determined by industry, function, or product or service. Rather the key factors are the nature of the work and its performance challenges, the people doing the work and their values, the need for large-scale cooperation, and the readiness of the people to be both entrepreneurial and collaborative at the same time. The essential condition for good fit is people's openness to collaboration and their readiness to structure their collaboration through reasoned and transparent, yet passionate, deliberation. The traditional hierarchical firm may function well enough when work is routine, systematic, and calls on largely unskilled labor. But as all companies become more knowledge-intensive, as they take on the challenge to add more value through better and more motivated talent, self-governing citizen approaches will come to fit an increasingly wide range of enterprises.

Size

The third architectural variable is size: How big is the organization now and how big does it seek to become? To date, most successful experiments in "workplace democracy" have been with small, "village-sized" organizations or business units—for example, St. Luke's advertising agency, the Oticon strategic management group, and a GE jet-engine plant in North Carolina.[9] In these organizations, most meaningful decision making can be made through face-to-face deliberations among people who know one another well and have learned to trust one another's judgment on the basis of extensive direct and mutual experience. A few other well-known examples of participative management—for example, W. L. Gore & Associates—are much larger, but none of the examples known to us is either as large or fully self-governing as ancient Athenian democracy.[10]

The success of the Athenian model, as we saw, was its capacity to be simultaneously big *and* small, to scale up from the level of the village by building master people networks consisting of multiple, smaller face-to-face networks, thereby leveraging knowledge and relationships across large populations and relatively long distances. The Athenian experience demonstrates that, even without employing sophisticated communications technology, the company of citizens solution can be adapted to operating units consisting of several tens of thousands of persons without strain. That would in fact cover most firms today: For example, only five of the companies listed in *Fortune's* "100 Best Companies to Work for in America" currently employ more than 50,000 people.[11]

If, however, the Athenian model suggests the possibility of relatively large companies of citizens, it does not mean that every contemporary experiment of this sort should aim for the same scale. A citizen-style model might be appropriate to only part of a larger organization (indeed many of the best executive leadership teams implicitly follow many of the Athenian values and practices); or it might be adapted to more limited organizational forms that cut across boundaries of traditional firms (for example, the governance of certain kinds of alliances and cooperatives, or the governance of a community of practice).[12] On the other hand, any aspiration to create a large-scale company of citizens must recognize the power of the participatory practice of "networking networks"—starting small and expanding upon familiar relationships to build up a more diverse and larger community of citizens over time. As communications and coordinating technology continue to evolve, the potential to reach even larger-scale citizen organizations is likely to increase—although given the continued importance of periodic face-to-face interactions, we can't necessarily assume that the potential for scale is infinitely large.

Membership

The fourth variable, membership, raises the most important question that the builders of a company of citizens must answer. The membership question is simple enough to express—"Who will be a 'citizen' in the company?"—but challenging to determine and manage in practice. What does membership actually mean for a given group? What are the benefits, rights, and responsibilities that go along with full membership? Should there be lesser rights and responsibilities for those who hold partial membership, or for people on whose work the organization depends but who are really not appropriate to be members at all? How should these different statuses of "belonging" be managed?

As we saw, the Athenians drew a strong line between native adult males (who were full citizens) and everyone else in the society and extended enterprise (who were not citizens)—and they did so ultimately to their own detriment. So how can modern leaders of companies of citizens find the right balance? They realize that they need to achieve scale by aligning as many highly motivated, self-governing people as possible. But just where is the point of diminishing returns? How can they avoid the slide into meaninglessness and cynicism that must come from pretending that everyone in any way involved with an enterprise is a full member of the organization as a community? And how also to avoid the chaos that would predictably follow upon suddenly conferring "self-governance" among thousands of unprepared people?

Those questions can be answered in part by paying proper attention to differences between citizenship in the modern firm and in the ancient city. As full-fledged citizens of the city-state of Athens, ancient Athenians were expected to owe no loyalty to any other political entity: They were culturally Greeks, but not citizens of Greece—indeed Greece did not yet exist as a nation.

By way of contrast, at least for the foreseeable future, modern organizational citizens are likely also to remain legal citizens of a nation-state, subject to and protected by national laws that ultimately have precedence over many of the rules and customs of their firm. Moreover, unlike the Athenian who lived and died as one who belonged to his native city (and generally could not be "fired" from his position as citizen), modern workers are not likely to imagine that their commitment to any given organization will last indefinitely: probably not for a lifetime and certainly not for that of their descendants. A company of citizens should not be confused with traditional Japanese firms; it does not necessarily imply a promise of "lifetime employment" (from employer) or blind devotion (from employee) to a paternalistic enterprise.

Finally, the modern worker may, without seeming treasonous, owe loyalty to more than one organization simultaneously—for example, both to a for-profit firm from which she receives a salary and to a not-for-profit organization that promotes a cause she believes in. Moreover, within the world of business, free agents and part-time workers typically "belong" (at some level) to multiple organizations. This sort of multiplicity of loyalties means that most modern organizational citizens are not willing (or even able) to offer up their lives for a one and only company— but by the same token, that high level of sacrifice need not be expected from every worker in order to guarantee a modern company's success. Because the modern individual is likely to have membership in various organizations (including a nation-state), the architecture of citizenship in a modern organization must be more flexible than it was in the city of ancient Athens. Including more people in modern organizational self-governance does not necessarily dilute benefits for each member. At the same time, limiting full citizenship in today's organization need not exclude those who are not regarded as citizens from access to membership in other organizations, nor does it compromise their fundamental human rights.

As we have emphasized, ancient Athens faced graver performance challenges than do modern firms—often, literally, the
survival of its members. So it necessarily demanded a higher
level of commitment and sacrifice from its members—often, literally, a willingness to die for the preservation of one's family and
fellow citizens. In exchange, the organization offered a lifetime
and multigenerational commitment to each citizen. The modern
company of citizens is quite capable of flourishing for an extended period of time without demanding an undivided commitment from its workers.

As a consequence, for a modern firm, the answer to the
question "Who is a member?" need not be driven by answering
the question "Who is willing to offer us *total* commitment?"
Rather, membership will be offered to those who are willing to
offer the *necessary level* of commitment and who also possess the
necessary talents. Just what that necessary level of commitment
and talent will entail for any given organization will vary considerably according to the business context, market conditions,
and some agreed-upon notion of culture, "work-life balance,"
and definition of the actual commitment expected. Membership, in all the richness discussed in this book, is yet another design choice that will be part of what we have called the overall
architecture of citizenship.

Deciding who will actually be a citizen is among the most
important issues in building a citizen company. The bar cannot
be set so low as to allow virtually anyone, however related to the
firm, to be a full member, regardless of his or her commitment or
abilities. Without establishing some clearly defined boundaries—some minimum assumed level of commitment and capability—the concept of citizenship becomes meaningless. When
the standard is lax, the words "the people are the company"

devolve to a mere slogan, fit perhaps for an annual report but not reflective of lived experience of actual workers.

On the other hand, if the bar is set too high, if the boundary is drawn too narrowly and only a small percentage of the people in a firm are regarded as its "members," the organization becomes an oligarchy (or reverts to the all-too-familiar *de facto* Industrial Age hierarchy). If this happens, the advantages of knowledge sharing, engagement, and trust building, typical of participatory democratic citizenship, are lost. We do not suggest that every person whose work supports a company must necessarily be a citizen, but if one desires to build such a community, then a substantial number certainly should be: The history of Athens shows that failing to expand the citizen body can lead to failure when the organization confronts unexpected new challenges and dangerous rivals. Finding the right balance between exclusiveness and inclusiveness—while preserving an overall democratic ethos—calls for candid conversation, thoughtful planning and experimentation, and graceful management of talent.

A big part of managing the membership variable of the citizenship architecture is to develop clear principles and processes by which an individual actually becomes a full member—and then to embed those principles and processes in the ongoing structural evolution of the company.[13] The lessons from the Athenian model suggest that the privileges of citizenship must reflect a corresponding responsibility on the part of the citizen: It is an honor that is properly conferred on worthy individuals through a decision of the citizens themselves.

Those lessons also suggest that the coherence of the citizen community depends on its "both/and" ability to preserve its sense of special membership, while simultaneously extending a spectrum of other kinds of membership to broader and broader circles of "knowledgeable belonging." Successful organizations in the future—equipped with new communications technology, flexible work arrangements, and global opportunities that Athenians never knew—will push the boundaries of defining a "citizen community" far beyond what the ancient *politeia* ever envisioned.

One way to clarify the question of who is a citizen is to accept the proposition that citizens should have a material stake in the firm. With regard to distribution of rewards, members of the organization need to be, in a meaningful sense, co-owners of the success that they collectively create—as well as coresponsible for failure. The realignment of a firm around self-governing citizen-workers may, for example, be enhanced by offering stock ownership to the members, building on the trend already in the marketplace of providing stock options and share purchase incentives. But as the collapse of Enron in 2001 and similar scandals in other companies have made glaringly obvious, stock options for employees can turn out to be a cruel deceit when the company's culture is not based on transparency, accountability, challenge, and earned trust. After the collapse of companies such as Enron and so many "new economy" Internet and telecommunications companies, we have to imagine that knowledge workers will be less eager to grant their loyalty in exchange for stock options unless they have a real role in making and monitoring decisions that affect their stake.

In his recent work on "business citizenship," Charles Handy noted the anomaly of organizations whose value is increasingly based on the talent and knowledge work of their people, but whose ownership is largely in the hands of outside investors—a structural paradox for public companies that depend on investment from capital markets. Like us, he believes that anomaly will become less tolerable in years ahead, and he reflects on how the paradox might be resolved. He suggests a future in which companies of citizens will issue two classes of shares—voting shares for members of the company (and some major stakeholders) and nonvoting shares for more casual or short-term investors; thus citizenship is rewarded with both economic and voting rights in the company.[14] Handy's suggestion is likely to be but one of a range of different passive and active ownership structures that will emerge in the future. The important point is that the people whose talent and knowledge work create the value of their organizations must come to center stage in terms of rewards and honors. When *the company is the people,* people become a primary, not secondary, focus for organizational attention. Tougher and more transparent responsibilities and accountabilities will counterbalance the increased rewards and honors—the kind of duties that are willingly embraced by citizens and come with membership in a self-governing organization.

Meanwhile, along with paying attention to the rights and responsibilities associated with membership, leaders will need to identify and manage analogous packages for "noncitizen" and "less-than-full citizen" members of the wider organizational society. Appropriate rights and responsibilities must be considered not only for those with "employee status," but also for part-timers, freelancers, and temporaries, and potentially also for members of the extended enterprise with whom more and more organizations collaborate and partner: allies, channels, suppliers, investors, and even customers. A company of citizens must understand what roles such constituencies play in shaping and maintaining what the core organization stands for and achieves. Membership is a critical architectural input across a wide range of meanings.

In many ways, the question of who is a citizen is already confronting most organizations today. Companies distinguish "professional staff" from "support staff," "employees" from "contractors," "our people" from "our alliance partners"—but the boundaries are often difficult to maintain, and in fast-paced, fluid economies, boundaries will continue to change and evolve. As all organizations become more knowledge-based and more democratic and as they integrate across boundaries with others, a distinguishing competence of companies of citizens will be the ability to manage dynamically different membership roles, providing the right balance of rights and responsibilities to the right groups of people, and finding ways to extend the spirit of citizenship more broadly, without diminishing its meaning and purpose to the critical core of the citizens themselves.

Leadership

Leadership is the fifth variable for the architecture of citizenship. Are the organization's leaders ready to "rule and be ruled in turns," by sharing the responsibilities and the rewards of governance? Do they regard building leadership capabilities in others as part of their leadership role? Are leaders ready to accept accountability and listen to challenges from their own people? In this book we have defined the concept of leadership broadly and in a democratic sense, because a company of citizens cannot be built entirely by the efforts of a small group of enlightened executives; the full community of committed citizens must also build it themselves. As we have stressed in previous chapters, the work of creating such a community is a process of building values, structures, and practices through the experience of both "doing and learning citizenship"—at all levels.

Leadership must become a shared responsibility, but launching and building a company of citizens will take initiative and inspiration from a committed leadership group, and the continuing evolution of the community will require an ongoing supply of people who can stand before their colleagues, articulate the community's values, drive its institutions and practices, and motivate others to embrace them. The Athenian case demonstrates the importance of visionary leaders such as Cleisthenes and Pericles, men who not only built their citizen culture through their own actions, but also inspired their fellow Athenians through their words and support to discover and actualize the power of that culture. Without leaders such as these, no organization will ever come to understand, much less achieve, the ethos and practice of citizenship. By its nature, however, the company of citizens involves risk and change for all potential members, and leadership roles must be available throughout the community. Thus in building such a community, people must understand their own and their colleagues' potential; citizens must have an accurate sense of each potential leader's ability to drive change and readiness to put him or herself "on the line."

The variable of leadership must stress, for all in authority or who would take on authority, readiness both to rule and be ruled. Citizens must be prepared to step up to leadership challenges, and leaders must be prepared to yield control to others, in due course—following the practice of rotation. The necessity for leaders to give up power as the community develops is among the greatest barriers to building a company of citizens from an existing hierarchical organization. Not surprisingly, even highly progressive, participative-management companies often continue to operate under the guiding umbrella of an "enlightened founder" or guardian executives.[15] Their communities are made up of self-governing citizens, but only up to a certain point.

The full rotation of leadership may in fact seem a major barrier for many organizations seeking to build a robust company of citizens. Advocates of change will confront the fact that for public companies, investors and shareholders are often "betting on the CEO," and thus such advocates must also confront the fact that capital markets have not historically welcomed a regularly changing cast of executives. However, shareholders themselves may already be driving a new approach to leadership in public companies. Given the increasing frequency with which CEOs are now forced to step down, it appears that the market is beginning to impose on companies what self-governing citizens themselves know: Regular changes of leadership, though sometimes painful, are often the best guarantee of fresh ideas and management approaches, and can minimize cronyism and self-entitlement.[16]

In seeking to build a company of citizens, advocates must carefully assess the quality of the community's leadership, both current and potential. A key factor will be whether the most prominent leaders are ready to align themselves with the practices of a self-governing community—including accountability, transparency, and rotation. An important complementary factor is whether the community has the right scale and potential talent to provide for an ongoing rotation.

Organizational Maturity

The sixth and final variable to consider in the architecture of citizenship is organizational maturity: How far along, and in what ways, has the organization in question developed? How developed (or entrenched) are the culture of community and the processes of governance? Are people willing to change? What will it take to transform the organization's existing culture and practices to those of a citizen community?

Building a company of citizens will be a different experience for leaders of established companies than it will be for leaders of start-ups or other "greenfield" situations. In general, in established companies, the deeper and more familiar the old ways of doing business, the more difficult the task of creating a citizen transformation. The barriers, however, can be both mental and habitual. If people in a company have never known any kind of self-governance or democracy, if that lack of experience in self-governance extends to their daily lives and upbringing, the prospects for change will be very challenging indeed.

We should recall, however, that Cleisthenes and his Athenian colleagues faced their own set of high barriers to change and overcame some deeply established ways of doing business in 508 B.C. It was a life-or-death performance demand—saving the city—that catalyzed the great citizen revolution of Athens. Faced with a mature organization set in its ways, the leaders of a would-be company of citizens must take advantage of performance challenges to focus change and learn to combine revolution with evolution. They will mix a "jolt to the system" with experimentally introducing citizen values and processes, likely starting small and building skills and practices through active participatory processes that can be extended and grown over time.

The start-up or greenfield enterprise offers the leader a chance to recruit people whose values and commitments are already suited both to taking on the risks and earning the rewards of citizenship. Institutions can be designed from the start with democratic values in mind, and thereby avoid the often painful problems of legacy thinking and acting. But that is not to say that building a company of citizens from scratch will be a simple matter. We have stressed throughout this book the importance of closely integrating values with structure and practices. Developing all three dimensions of the citizenship triad requires discipline and focus—two things that are usually in short supply during the early stages of a new company's formation; the inevitable cry from many will be to postpone the organizational work until later. In certain cases, their impulse may be right; much depends on both short-term and longer-term priorities and performance requirements. There is a trade-off in any organization between the advantages of legacy—having a secure platform from which to build change—and the advantages of greenfield—not having to deal with the costs and risks of people unlearning established beliefs and behaviors. There is no all-purpose answer here.

Success in achieving a truly self-governing citizen organization will require a commitment to pursuing its potential, and a willingness to invest significant time and attention for the longer-term value and performance it can potentially enable. Those willing to embark on the journey will do so believing in the power of people and the greater value that can be created if people are allowed to take charge of themselves and become truly accountable for their own collective success and failure. When and how to begin that kind of transformation will depend on when leaders and workers alike are ready to embrace the responsibilities and opportunities of self-governance.

IN THE COURSE of this book, we have told the story of a high-performing and innovative organizational system invented by the ancient Athenians. It is a system that had a unique historical setting, yet it is timelessly familiar for what it achieved: building enduring monuments to excellence while giving people the power to steer their own destiny and also achieve high performance. The means by which the Athenians accomplished that was an ingenious culture of community that unified and balanced democratic values, structures of governance, and participatory practices.

We have argued that this system is adaptable to today's organizations, compensating for obvious differences between ancient cities and modern firms, and understanding that every organization must find its own way and approach to the business needs it addresses. Building a company of citizens will not be the right solution for every situation, but we believe that it will be increasingly right for an ever-wider range of situations in the future. We base that conviction on the assumption that business and other enterprises are becoming ever more knowledge-based, ever more dependent on their people. And that will mean that leaders will struggle more than ever to resolve the increasingly urgent paradox of building the scale of a fully aligned community while simultaneously encouraging the freedom and equality of entrepreneurial individuals. In an era of increasing appreciation for democracy, as a system of governance and as a set of values, we should not be surprised to find citizen-style practices reborn in the workplaces of the global economy.

But that will not happen magically, impersonally, or without effort; nor is success guaranteed. It will require pioneers and leaders who will rise to the challenge of building very new kinds of organizations by creatively adapting the framework of an ancient community, people who are willing to accept the risks of doing so—in anticipation of rewards that, in the beginning, will only be potential. The journey will not be brief. In the end, however, the measure of success will not be the speed with which these kinds of organizations are created, but rather their performance, agility, vitality, and potential for self-renewal over time. The history of the Athenian model shows that an organization in which people are treated as citizens, and treat one another as such, can indeed produce those desirable outcomes. Whether it is the right model for your company, only you can decide.

Notes

Preface

1. Charles Handy, *The Hungry Spirit* (New York: Broadway Books, 1998), 171–172.

Chapter 1

1. At more than 26,000 square feet, the Parthenon as it stands today is a huge building. Eighty-five great columns, each thirty-three feet tall, support a complex superstructure, including massive pediments and elegantly sculptured metopes. Measurements and quotation: William B. Dinsmoor, *The Architecture of Ancient Greece* (New York: Norton, 1975), 164.
2. Ibid., 165.
3. Quote: R.E. Wycherley, *The Stones of Athens* (Princeton, NJ: Princeton University Press, 1978), 125.
4. Thucydides, *The Peloponnesian War*, 2.31, trans. Rex Warner (New York: Viking Penguin, 1972). Translation slightly revised by the authors. Reproduced by permission of Penguin Books Ltd. All subsequent quotations from Thucydides' history will be from this translation, are slightly revised by the authors, and are used with permission of Penguin Books Ltd. Citations refer to the traditional "book" and "section(s)" of the text, which are clearly indicated in the Penguin edition, rather than to page numbers.

5. Compare the discussion of human-centric organizations in Charles O'Reilly and Jeffrey Pfeffer, *Hidden Value: How Great Companies Achieve Extraordinary Results with Ordinary People* (Boston: Harvard Business School Press, 2000).

6. The historical fact that only men were Athenian citizens has governed our decision throughout the book to refer to citizens using male pronouns (e.g., "his values," "what it meant to him") when referring to Athens. We do not mean to suggest prescriptively that women were not historically worthy to be citizens, nor that they shouldn't be treated and counted as citizens in the new organizational model we present. Our views on the desirability of gender-neutral considerations of "citizen rights and responsibilities" should be adequately clear throughout.

7. We discuss this issue in more detail in chapter 6.

8. There is a vast literature on "organizations of the future," which we won't attempt to cite in detail here. A good introduction to many of the more recent models and concepts, with a bibiliography, is Charles Leadbeater, *The Weightless Society* (New York and London: Texere, 2000). See also Peter Drucker, "Will the Corporation Survive?" *The Economist,* 3 November 2001, 14–18; Peter Drucker, "The Future of the Company," *The Economist,* 22 December 2001; John Micklethwaite and Adrian Woolridge, *The Witch Doctors* (New York: Times Books, 1996), 95–121; and Tom Peters, *Liberation Management: Necessary Disorganization in the Nanosecond Nineties* (New York: Knopf, 1992), 129.

9. Opening statement of *The Social Contract,* quoted in John Rawls, *The Law of Peoples* (Cambridge: Harvard University Press, 1999), 13.

10. Best discussed in his recent work, Peter Drucker, *Post-Capitalist Society* (New York: Harper Business, 1993), 6.

11. This point and many others related to our discussion can be found in the brief but important article by John Seely Brown and Estee Solomon-Gray, "The People Are the Company," *Fast Company,* November 1995, 78–82.

12. For some interesting reflections on the modern impulse to search for meaning and values outside of traditional institutions such as schools and churches, see Alan Wolf, "The Final Freedom," *New York Times Magazine,* 18 March 2001, 48–51.

13. We are well aware that the case has already been made many times, both in theory and practice, about the value of "participative management" in the Knowledge Economy, and more generally about the contemporary trend toward "workplace democracy." Our discussion, looking at the very special and appropriate model of the ancient Athenian democratic city-state, intends to complement, and indeed draw strength from, the growing literature and studies of "democratic organizations." Good starting points for those are: Charles Manz and Henry Simms Jr, *Business Without Bosses* (New York: Wiley & Sons, 1995); Russell Ackoff, *The Democratic Corporation* (New York: Oxford University Press, 1994); Patricia McLagan and Christo Nel, *The Age of Participation* (San Francisco: Berrett-Koehler Publishers, 1995 and 1997); Ronald E. Purser and Steve Cabana, *The Self-Managing Organization* (New York: Free Press, 1998); and Warren Bennis and Philip Slater, "Democracy is Inevitable," in *The Temporary Society: What Is Happening to Business and Family Life in America Under the Impact of Accelerating Change* (San Francisco: Jossey-Bass, 1998), 1–23. See also references in the notes of chapter 6.

　　Among the extensive literature on democratic theory, we have found especially stimulating: Benjamin Barber, *Strong Democracy: Participatory Politics for a New Age* (Berkeley: University of California Press, 1984); and Robert A. Dahl, *Democracy and its Critics* (New Haven, CT: Yale University Press, 1989).

Chapter 2

1. For a modern account of the Persian invasion of Greece, see Barry Strauss and Josiah Ober, *The Anatomy of Error* (New York: St. Martin's Press, 1990), chapter 1. The most authoritative ancient account is Herodotus, *The Histories,* written approximately two generations after the events.
2. Thucydides, *The Peloponnesian War,* 1.89–117, offers a succinct and near-contemporary account of the growth and structure of the Athenian overseas empire; for more information see Malcolm McGregor, *The Athenians and their Empire* (Vancouver: University of British Columbia Press, 1987).

3. For further information, see Anthony J. Podlecki, *The Life of Themistocles* (New York: Ares Publishers, 1975).

4. See, for example, Gretchen Morgenson, "Pushing the Pay Envelope Too Far," *New York Times,* 14 April 2002. For a much needed correction to the contemporary notion that leaders must be overcompensated heroic figures, see Jim Collins, *Good to Great: Why Some Companies Make the Leap and Others Don't* (New York: HarperCollins, 2001).

5. On Pericles and his political career, see Donald Kagan, *Pericles of Athens and the Birth of Democracy* (New York: Free Press, 1998).

6. For demographic estimates, see Mogens H. Hansen, *Demography and Democracy: The Number of Athenian Citizens in the Fourth Century B.C.* (Herning, Denmark: Systime, 1986).

7. The history of this idea is discussed in depth in Jennifer Roberts, *Athens on Trial: The Antidemocratic Tradition in Western Thought* (Princeton, NJ: Princeton University Press, 1994).

8. For further information, see Edward E. Cohen, *Athenian Economy and Society: A Banking Perspective* (Princeton, NJ: Princeton University Press, 1992) and *The Athenian Nation* (Princeton, NJ: Princeton University Press, 2000).

The story of Pasion and his family also underlines the fact, which must be faced squarely, that Athens was a slave-owning society (though the extent and economic significance of the institution is debated; see Chester Starr, "An Overdose of Slavery," *Journal of Economic History* 18 [1958]: 17–30). Despite their many advances, the Athenians never seriously contemplated the abolition of slavery and the life of a slave was not a pleasant one. But by the same token, slavery in Athens was neither as cruelly oppressive nor as socially divisive as the race-based slavery of the New World.

9. Thucydides, *The Peloponnesian War,* 1.70–71.

10. Ibid., 1.71.

11. Pericles' Funeral Oration is reported in ibid., 2.35–46.

12. On "both/and" thinking, see P. Brook Manville, "Pericles and the 'both/and' Vision for Democratic Athens," in *Polis and Polemos,* ed. Charles D. Hamilton and Peter Krentz (Claremont, CA: Regina Books, 1997), 73–84; and James C. Collins and Jerry I. Porras, *Built to Last: Successful Habits of Visionary Companies* (New York: Harper-Collins, 1994), 44–45.

13. The great plague, described by Thucydides, *The Peloponnesian War*, 2.47–55, has never been securely associated with any known modern disease. Phormio's campaign in the Corinthian Gulf: Thucydides, *The Peloponnesian War*, 2.79–92.

14. See Barry S. Strauss, "Democracy, Kimon, and the Evolution of Athenian Naval Tactics in the Fifth Century B.C," in *Polis and Politics*, ed. P. Flensted-Jensen, T. H. Neilsen, and L. Rubinstein (Copenhagen: Museum Tusculanum Press, 2000), 315–326. Strauss notes that not all Athenian rowers were citizens, but that citizen values permeated naval training and united the interests of citizens and noncitizens onboard the ships.

15. Cross-appropriation: Charles Spinosa, Fernando Flores, and Hubert L. Dreyfus, *Disclosing New Worlds: Entrepreneurship, Democratic Action, and the Cultivation of Solidarity* (Cambridge, MA: MIT Press, 1997).

16. See the survey in Jürgen Kluge, Wolfram Stein, and Thomas Licht, *Knowledge Unplugged: The McKinsey & Company Global Survey on Knowledge Management* (New York: Palgrave Macmillan, 2001). For examples of "democratic culture organizations" today, see references in chapter 1, note 11, and further in chapter 6.

Chapter 3

1. For a more detailed treatment of the emergence of Athenian citizenship, and the reforms for Solon and Cleisthenes, see P. Brook Manville, *The Origins of Citizenship in Ancient Athens* (Princeton, NJ: Princeton University Press, 1997), and the literature cited therein.

2. Solon, Fragment 36, preserved in Aristotle, *The Constitution of the Athenians*, 12.4. Our translation.

3. For a full narrative and analysis, see Josiah Ober, *The Athenian Revolution* (Princeton, NJ: Princeton University Press, 1996), chapter 5. The most authoritative ancient accounts are Herodotus, *Histories*, 5.66–73, and Aristotle, *The Constitution of the Athenians*, 20–22.

4. For further discussion of freedom and equality as cultural norms, see chapter 4.

5. This goal is confirmed by Aristotle in *The Constitution of the Athenians*, 21.2.

6. Networking of people networks, and other key practices of citizenship, are discussed in detail in chapter 5.

7. Peter J. Rhodes, *The Athenian Boule* (Oxford: Clarendon Press, 1985) offers a comprehensive account of the Council of 500. The structure and work of this Council is discussed further in chapter 4.

8. For further discussion of the numbers of Athenians and their rate of service on the Council, see Mogens H. Hansen, *Demography and Democracy: The Number of Athenian Citizens in the Fourth Century B.C.* (Herning, Denmark: Systime, 1986).

9. Deliberately limiting the size of business units is a practice observed in many professional services firms (for example, McKinsey & Co., as noted by Manville during his tenure there, 1987–1998); it is also seen in various other kinds of large corporate organizations. Representative cases include Asea Brown Boveri (Tom Peters, *Liberation Management* [New York: Knopf, 1992], 44–55); General Electric (Jack Welch, *Jack: Straight From the Gut* [New York: Warner Business Books, 2001], 398–399); and Dell (particularly during the 1990s: interview by Manville with Robert Knaggs, Global Learning Technology Manager, Dell Corporation, June 2002).

Chapter 4

1. Pericles' Funeral Oration (as recorded by Thucydides, *The Peloponnesian War,* 2.35–46) and its celebration of Athenian citizenship values is discussed and quoted extensively in chapter 2.

2. Comment of the general Nicias to Athenian troops in Sicily, recorded by Thucydides, *The Peloponnesian War,* 7.77.

3. For a full discussion of the Athenian view of "law as educator" see Manville, *Origins of Citizenship,* 21; and Josiah Ober, "The Debate over Civic Education in Classical Athens," in *Education in Greek and Roman Antiquity,* ed. Yun Lee Too (Leiden, Netherlands: E.J. Brill, 2001), 273–305.

4. We discuss the great exception to the Athenian toleration of criticism, the trial of the philosopher Socrates, in chapter 5.

5. Wealthy Athenians paid more taxes, but the masses of ordinary citizens did not use their power of numbers to seize the goods of the

rich. Certain Athenians, notably the physically handicapped and children whose fathers had died in military campaigns, received what we would today call welfare benefits from the city. But there was never a sustained effort to redistribute wealth systematically across society in order to achieve economic parity among citizens. See further, Josiah Ober, *Mass and Elite in Democratic Athens* (Princeton, NJ: Princeton University Press, 1989), chapter 5.

6. Plato emphasizes Athenian respect for technical expertise in their public assemblies (citing as examples architects and naval specialists) in his dialogue *Protagoras,* 319b–d. Aristotle analyzes how the knowledge of many diverse people is aggregated in the process of democratic deliberations in his work *The Politics,* 1281a–b, 1286a. For further discussion, see David Keyt, "Aristotle's Theory of Distributive Justice," in *A Companion to Aristotle's Politics,* ed. Fred D. Miller and David Keyt (Oxford: B. Blackwell, 1991), 238–278.

7. Herodotus, *Histories,* 5.78.

8. Robert D. Putnam, *Making Democracy Work: Civic Traditions in Modern Italy* (Princeton, NJ: Princeton University Press, 1993) discusses the value of social capital in building effective communities, and the ways that it can be eroded by exploitative patron/client relations. On social capital in general in businesses, see also Don Cohen and Larry Prusak, *In Good Company: How Social Capital Makes Organizations Work* (Boston: Harvard Business School Press, 2001). On the absence of patronage in Athens, see Paul C. Millet, "Patronage and Its Avoidance in Classical Athens," in *Patronage in Ancient Society,* ed. A. Wallace Hadrill (London: Routledge, 1989), 15–48.

9. An excellent overview of the institutions of democracy in this period is offered by Mogens H. Hansen, *The Athenian Democracy in the Age of Demosthenes* (Norman, OK: University of Oklahoma Press, 1999).

10. An example is Agilent's ability to retain the enthusiastic support of their workers through periods of serious downsizing through "participatory management," which "succeeded in turning the 'us' vs. 'them' of corporate downsizing into just 'us.'" Robert Levering and Milton Moskowitz, "The Best in the Worst of Times," *Fortune,* 4 February 2002, 66. For other cases, see literature cited in chapter 1, note 12.

11. This is a paraphrase of the Athenian law against outrage (*hybris*), which is cited in full in Demosthenes' speech *Against Meidias,* 21.47.

For further discussion, see Josiah Ober, "Quasi-Rights: Political Boundaries and Social Diversity in Democratic Athens," *Social Philosophy and Policy* 17 (2000): 27–61.

12. Arbitrators, like other Athenian magistrates, were "experienced amateurs"; it was the duty of each citizen who reached age sixty to spend a year in this civic role. Many other disputes were settled by recourse to private arbitration. See further Virginia J. Hunter, *Policing Athens: Social Control in the Attic Lawsuits, 420–320 B.C.* (Princeton, NJ: Princeton University Press, 1994), 55–76.

13. A full account of the campaign is provided in Thucydides, *The Peloponnesian War*, 4.2–41.

14. Behind these kinds of estimates lies a wealth of scholarship and indeed more than a little controversy. For relevant discussions see Hansen, *Athenian Democracy*, 61–64, 79–81; Ober, *Mass and Elite*, 127–48; and Manville, *Origins of Citizenship*, 17–20.

15. The Assembly debate is described by Herodotus, *Histories*, 7.139–44. See chapter 2, note 1 for references to modern work on the Persian War background.

Chapter 5

1. This discussion owes much to Bill Snyder's good advice and to the important book he wrote with two colleagues: Etienne Wenger, Richard McDermott, and William M. Snyder, *Cultivating Communities of Practice: A Guide to Managing Knowledge* (Boston: Harvard Business School Press, 2002), 23–47. We have also been influenced by work of Anthony Giddens, *Central Problems in Social Theory* (Berkeley, CA: University of California Press, 1979).

2. Aristotle, *Politics*, 1274a22–1275b20.

3. Here we are following contemporary political theorists (notably Isaiah Berlin) in defining "positive right" as a right to engage in something desirable (to participate in ruling), in contrast to a "negative right" to be protected against something undesirable (for example, unwanted intrusion into private life). It is sometimes asserted that negative rights were unknown in ancient Greece, but see the essays

by Mogens H. Hansen, Robert W. Wallace, and Ellen M. Wood in *Demokratia: A Conversation on Democracies, Ancient and Modern,* ed. Josiah Ober and Charles Hedrick (Princeton, NJ: Princeton University Press, 1996).

4. On this problem, see Charles Handy, *The Hungry Spirit* (New York: Broadway Books, 1998), 171–172.

5. For a discussion of quorums and other mechanisms of ensuring participation, see Hansen, *Athenian Democracy,* 130–132.

6. This point has already been made many times by many insightful people before us. Illustrations and discussions can be found in, for example, Tom Davenport and Larry Prusak, *Working Knowledge: How Organizations Manage What They Know* (Boston: Harvard Business School Press, 1998), especially beginning on page 123; John Seely Brown and Paul Duguid, *The Social Life of Information* (Boston: Harvard Business School Press, 2000); and Michael Schrage, *Shared Minds: The New Technologies of Collaboration* (New York: Random House, 1990).

7. See for example Jon Katzenbach and Douglas K. Smith, *The Wisdom of Teams* (Boston: Harvard Business School Press, 1993), 130; Wenger, McDermott, and Snyder, *Cultivating Communities of Practice,* 107; and Don Tapscott, David Ticoll, and Alex Lowy, *Digital Capital: Harnessing the Power of Business Webs* (Boston: Harvard Business School Press, 2000), 134.

8. For thoughtful analysis of this problem, see Davenport and Prusak, *Working Knowledge,* 88; Brown and Duguid, *The Social Life of Information,* 117.

9. For discussion of the methods by which Athenian executive teams were selected, see Hansen, *Athenian Democracry,* 229–237.

10. For a good discussion of the essential role of deliberation for democratic decision making, see Amy Gutmann and Denis Thompson, *Democracy and Disagreement* (Cambridge: Harvard University Press, 1996).

11. For the absence of party politics in Athens and the nature of political groups there, see Barry S. Strauss, *Athens after the Peloponnesian War: Class, Faction and Policy 403–386 B.C.* (London: Croom Helm, 1986).

12. Thucydides, *The Peloponnesian War,* 2.39. See fuller discussion of this passage in the notes to chapter 2.

13. See for example, Francis Fukuyama, *Trust: The Social Virtues and the Creation of Prosperity* (New York: Free Press, 1996); and Cohen and Prusak, *In Good Company*.

14. See discussion in Ober, *Mass and Elite,* 138.

15. Ibid., 177–182

16. As recounted by the ancient biographer Plutarch, *Life of Demosthenes,* 6–8.

17. On the career of Aeschines, see E. M. Harris, *Aeschines and Athenian Politics* (New York: Oxford University Press, 1995). For the changing sociology of leadership in democratic Athens, see W. Robert Connor, *The New Politicians of Fifth-Century Athens* (Princeton, NJ: Princeton University Press, 1971).

18. The incident is discussed in Demosthenes' lawcourt speech, number 21, *Against Meidias*. See discussion in Josiah Ober, *The Athenian Revolution,* chapter 7.

19. On the naturalization process, see Hansen, *Athenian Democracy,* 94–95.

20. The story of the trial and Socrates' decision to accept punishment is told in Plato's dialogues *Apology* and *Crito*. For further discussion, see Josiah Ober, *Political Dissent in Democratic Athens* (Princeton, NJ: Princeton University Press, 1998), 165–89.

21. See references in chapter 1, note 12.

Chapter 6

1. For the full story, see Christian Habicht, *Athens from Alexander to Antony* (Cambridge: Harvard University Press, 1997).

2. It is worth noting that the two hundred plus years of Athenian democracy—and their sustained innovation and high performance—goes far beyond the "horizons of success" (e.g., membership in the Fortune 500 or sustained higher-than-stock-market returns) of most modern companies—which are usually measured in decades at most. For a good discussion of the ephemeral nature of success in contemporary business organizations, see Collins and Porras, *Built to Last,* and Jim Collins, *Good to Great: Why Some Companies Make the*

Leap and Others Don't (NewYork: HarperCollins, 2001); also Richard
Foster and Sarah Kaplan, *Creative Destruction: Why CompaniesThatAre
Built to Last Underperform the Market—and How to Transform Them*
(NewYork: Doubleday, 2001).

3. In addition to cases included in the literature cited in chapter 1, note
12, we point to other noteworthy examples—all reflecting some
kind of distinctive performance—such as W. L. Gore & Associates, St.
Luke's advertising agency, the Durham, North Carolina, jet engine
plant of General Electric, Whole Foods Supermarkets, Oticon (the
Danish hearing aids manufacturer), Springfield Re-Manufacturing,
the "conductorless" Orpheus Chamber Orchestra, the association of
banks that make up Visa, and a variety of professional, business, and
European cooperatives. On W. L. Gore & Associates, see John Huey,
"The New Post-Heroic Leadership," *Fortune,* 21 February 1994,
42–50; and Michael Kaplan, " . . .You Have No Boss," *Fast Company*
11 (October/November 1997), 226. Further insights were provided
to Manville by interviews in 2001 with David S. Clarke, former CIO
of W. L. Gore. On St. Luke's advertising agency, see Leadbeater, *The
Weightless Society,* 68–71. On the Durham jet engine plant, see
Charles Fishman, "Engines of Democracy," *Fast Company* 28 (October 1999), 174. On Whole Foods, see Charles Fishman, "Whole
Foods is All Teams," *Fast Company* 2 (April 1996), 103. On Oticon,
see Thomas E. Vollman, *The Transformation Imperative* (Boston: Harvard Business School Press, 1996); Jürgen Kluge, Wolfram Stein, and
Thomas Licht, *Knowledge Unplugged:The McKinsey & Company Global
Survey on Knowledge Management* (New York: Palgrave Macmillan,
2001); and Polly Labarre, "The Dis-Organization of Oticon," *Industry Week,* 18 July 1994, 22. On Springfield Re-Manufacturing, see
Jack Stack, *The Great Game of Business* (NewYork: Currency Doubleday, 1994). On the Orpheus ensemble, see Harvey Seifter, Peter
Economy, and J. Richard Hackman, *Leadership Ensemble: Lessons in
Collaborative Management from the World's Only Conductorless Orchestra*
(NewYork: Henry Holt, 2001). On the members-owned organization
of Visa, see Dee Hock, *The Birth of the Chaordic Age* (San Francisco:
Berrett-Koehler, 1999). On cooperative membership organizations,
see discussions and examples provided by the National Cooperative

Business Association at <http://www.ncba.org>. On earlier experiments with democratic workplaces, see E. S. Greenberg, *Workplace Democracy: The Political Effects of Participation* (Ithaca, NY: Cornell University Press, 1986).

4. Peter Cappelli, *The New Deal at Work: Managing the Market-Driven Workforce* (Boston: Harvard Business School Press, 1999); Daniel H. Pink, *Free Agent Nation: How America's New Independent Workers Are Transforming the Way We Live* (New York: Warner Books, 2001); Bennis and Slater, *The Temporary Society;* and Leadbeater, *The Weightless Society.*

5. Drucker, *Post-Capitalist Society,* 74–82.

6. For more on teledemocracy, see Christa D. Slaton, *Televote: Expanding Citizen Participation in the Quantum Age* (New York: Praeger, 1992); Lawrence K. Grossman, *The Electronic Republic: Reshaping Democracy in the Information Age* (New York: Viking, 1995); and Dick Morris, *Vote.com* (Los Angeles, CA: Renaissance Books, 1999).

7. On virtual communities and issues related to technologically networked versus face-to-face relationships, see Nitin Nohria and Robert Eccles, "Face to Face: Making Network Organizations Work," in Nitin Nohria and Robert C. Eccles, *Networks and Organizations: Structure, Form, and Action* (Boston: Harvard Business School Press, 1992), 208–288; John Hagel and Arthur Armstrong, *Net Gain: Expanding Markets Through Virtual Communities* (Boston: Harvard Business School Press, 1997); and Wenger, McDermott, and Snyder, *Cultivating Communities of Practice,* 113–138. For a thoughtful political theorist's take on the relationship between citizenship and the Internet, see Cass R. Sunstein, *Republic.com* (Princeton, NJ: Princeton University Press, 2001).

8. For example, the GE jet engine plant, W. L. Gore & Associates, and Springfield Re-Manufacturing, cited above, note 2. See also Renée Mauborgne and W. Chan Kim, "Fair Process: Managing in the Knowledge Economy," *Harvard Business Review* 97 (July–August 1997): 65–75, on Miller Brewing and the Sparrows Point plant of Bethlehem Steel. See also Samuel Bowles and Herbert Gintis, *Democracy and Capitalism* (New York: Basic Books, 1986).

9. For references, see note 2 above.

10. On W. L. Gore & Associates, see note 2 above.

11. The five are AmEx (58,000 employees), FedEx (162,000), Publix Super Markets (118,000), Marriot (131,000), and Wal-Mart (918,000). For a complete list, see: <http://www.fortune.com/lists/bestcompanies/index.html> (last accessed 26 July 2002).

12. Tapscott, Ticoll, and Lowy, *Digital Capital,* 176–181; and Wenger, McDermott, and Snyder, *Cultivating Communities of Practice,* 126. Information on cooperatives is from Manville's conversations about members of the National Cooperative Business Association with Byron Henderson Vice President, Coop Operations, NCBA, in June 2001; see also <http://www.ncba.org>.

13. Lack of clarity about how one becomes a citizen is an issue that plagues some highly participatory communities; for example the "conductorless" Orpheus Chamber Orchestra. (We owe this information to original research and interviews conducted by Nathan Arrington of Princeton University.) See also Wenger, McDermott, and Snyder, *Cultivating Communities of Practice,* 56–58, on differing membership profiles in communities of practice.

14. Charles Handy, *The Hungry Spirit* (New York: Broadway Books, 1998), 171–172.

15. Thus William and Viv Gore at W. L. Gore & Associates (per Manville's interview with David Clark, ex-CIO, 2001); for the GE jet engine plant described in *Fast Company* there is an overall supervisor who is not elected by plant members and remains accountable to GE corporate goals and processes (see chapter 6, note 2). For other examples of highly participative companies that are still managed by an ultimately hierarchical leadership structure, see Pfeffer, *Hidden Value.*

16. For example, David Leonhardt, "The Imperial Chief Executive Is Suddenly in the Cross Hairs," *New York Times,* 24 June 2002. This is a front-page article, citing the cases of Stephen Case of AOL, Jeffrey Immelt (successor at GE to Jack Welch), and other CEOs who are having their feet held to fire or have been sacked as a result of investor or stockholder dissatisfaction. Leonhardt notes the huge rise of compensation of top CEOs (from 70 times what the average worker is paid in 1985 to 410 times that average in 2001) and contrasts the star treatment top CEOs received in the 1990s with their beleaguered status in 2002.

Index

About the Authors

BROOK MANVILLE is Chief Learning Officer at Saba Software, a provider of software for enterprise-wide human capital development and management software and services solutions. He is responsible for research, thought leadership, and development of customer learning communities and also consults to clients on matters related to organizational learning strategies. Prior to his appointment at Saba, he was a partner and member of the leadership team of the Organization Practice at McKinsey & Co. and served as McKinsey's first Director of Knowledge Management. He has also been a professor of classics and history at Northwestern University.

Manville has consulted on organizational issues for several Fortune 500 companies and published widely on topics related to organization, knowledge management, and workplace learning. His articles have appeared in *Fast Company, Leader to Leader, MIT Sloan Management Review,* the *Harvard Business Review,* and other specialized industry publications. Manville is the author of *The Origins of Athenian Citizenship* (Princeton University Press, 1989). He can be reached at bmanville@saba.com or pbmanville@yahoo.com.

JOSIAH OBER is Magie Professor and former chairman of the Department of Classics at Princeton University, where he holds a joint appointment in the University Center for Human Values. He teaches courses in ancient and modern participatory democracy and has published books and articles on Greek democracy, law, war, citizenship, and other topics. His book *Mass and Elite in Democratic Athens* was awarded the Goodwin Award of Merit by the American Philological Association in 1989. His other books include *The Athenian Revolution, Political Dissent in Democratic Athens,* and *The Anatomy of Error: Ancient Military Disasters and Their Lessons for Modern Strategists* (with Barry Strauss). A full bibliography is available at www.princeton.edu/classics.

Ober has appeared in a number of television documentaries on ancient Greek civilization and served as codirector of a major public program organized by the American School of Classical Studies to celebrate the 2,500th anniversary of the invention of democracy in classical Athens. He can be reached at jober@princeton.edu.